BRITISH SCREEN STORIES

THE STORY OF VICTORIAN FILM

Bryony Dixon

THE BRITISH FILM INSTITUTE
Bloomsbury Publishing Plc
50 Bedford Square, London, WC1B 3DP, UK
1385 Broadway, New York, NY 10018, USA
29 Earlsfort Terrace, Dublin 2, Ireland

BLOOMSBURY is a trademark of Bloomsbury Publishing Plc

First published in Great Britain 2023 by Bloomsbury on behalf of the
British Film Institute
21 Stephen Street, London W1T 1LN
www.bfi.org.uk

The BFI is the lead organisation for film in the UK and the distributor of Lottery funds for film. Our mission is to ensure that film is central to our cultural life, in particular by supporting and nurturing the next generation of film-makers and audiences. We serve a public role which covers the cultural, creative and economic aspects of film in the UK.

Copyright © Bryony Dixon, 2023

Bryony Dixon has asserted her right under the Copyright, Designs and Patents Act, 1988, to be identified as author of this work.

For legal purposes the Acknowledgements on p. 5 constitute an extension of this copyright page.

Cover design: Louise Dugdale
Front cover image: James Williamson's *The Big Swallow* (1901)

All rights reserved. No part of this publication may be reproduced or transmitted in any form or by any means, electronic or mechanical, including photocopying, recording, or any information storage or retrieval system, without prior permission in writing from the publishers.

Bloomsbury Publishing Plc does not have any control over, or responsibility for, any third-party websites referred to or in this book. All internet addresses given in this book were correct at the time of going to press. The author and publisher regret any inconvenience caused if addresses have changed or sites have ceased to exist, but can accept no responsibility for any such changes.

A catalogue record for this book is available from the British Library.

A catalog record for this book is available from the Library of Congress.

ISBN: PB: 978-1-9112-3961-1
HB: 978-1-9112-3962-8
ePDF: 978-1-9112-3964-2
ePUB: 978-1-9112-3963-5

Series: British Screen Stories

Designed, typeset and packaged by Tom Cabot/ketchup
Printed and bound in India

To find out more about our authors and books visit www.bloomsbury.com and sign up for our newsletters.

CONTENTS

    Acknowledgements. 5
    British Screen Stories: Editors' Introduction. 6
    Introduction: Time Recorded. 8
    Montage: Meet the Pioneers 18

1. 'Novelty? It's as old as the hills': Film and the Music Hall . 20
    Close-up: The Victorian Film Catalogue 32

2. 'Two Hundred Lies a Minute': Actuality and News . . . 34
    Close-up: Black Victorians 48

3. Here and Now: Topicals and Street Life 50
    Close-up: How to Identify Victorian Film 62

4. Everybody Marches: Military Films 64
    Close-up: The Pirates 80

5. The Greatest Draw: Local Film 82
    Close-up: The Kid Stays in the Picture 94

6. Moving Images: Panoramas, Phantom rides and Travel . 96
    Montage: The Phantom Ride 108
    Close-up: Researching Victorian film 110

7. New Perspectives: Art and Science 112
    Close-up: Picturing Ideas: The Victorian Commercial . . . 124

8.	Dancing on the Ceiling: Trick Films	126
9.	Larking About: Comedy	140
	Montage: *The Facial*	153
10.	Plays without Words: Drama and Adaptation	154
	Close-up: The Sound of Silents	168
	Epilogue: The End of all Things	170
	Tables	176
	Recommended Reading	177
	Notes	179
	Index	187
	Illustration Credits	191

ACKNOWLEDGEMENTS

First and foremost I would like to thank my BFI colleagues Mark Duguid and Patrick Russell for their highly engaged editorship and Rebecca Barden, Anna Coatman and Tom Cabot at Bloomsbury for their support. Thanks are also due to other BFI colleagues, including Robin Baker and Storm Patterson and many other curatorial colleagues, particularly Sonia Genaitay and Rebecca Vick, who sifted through the hundreds of elements of footage of Victoria's Jubilee and funeral. Numerous colleagues at the BFI Reuben Library (Ian O'Sullivan), BFI Southbank (Maggi Hurt and Johnathon Parkinson), BFI Player and at the BFI National Archive's Conservation Centre, who wrangled huge numbers of hard-to-identify Victorian films to make them accessible for the public and scholars in the UK. Thanks, too, to Adam Matthew Digital for extending access to these digitised films to international scholars. I am grateful to Tom Stevenson for some initial archival research, not least his hours spent identifying films of Queen Victoria's Diamond Jubilee from old photos.

My thanks go to the FIAF family, particularly staff of Eye Filmmuseum and MoMA. I am grateful to Camille Blot Wellens for help with images, and to all the experts in early film with whom I have chatted over the years about Victorian filmmaking – too many to name, but they include: Barry Anthony, Stephen Bottomore, Ian Christie, Frank Gray, Stephen Herbert, Joe Kember, Mariann Lewinsky, Luke McKernan, David Mayer, Helen Mayer, Deac Rossell, Vanessa Toulmin and Philip Wickham. Particular gratitude goes to Tony Fletcher, whose collections of documents on early film venues were of great help. Finally, special thanks go out to two late, great scholars: Richard Brown and Paul Spehr. And of course to family, friends and neighbours – thanks too.

BRITISH SCREEN STORIES: EDITORS' INTRODUCTION

A century and a quarter since the first films flickered onto the screen, moving images dominate our lives. Our workplaces, schools and homes – even the journeys between them – are saturated with film. So how did we get here? What's the story? Or rather, the *stories* – because film contains multitudes. Moving images preceded the cinema, found a new home on television, and began to fill the online space as soon as capacities allowed. Today, most of us carry a cinema in our pocket. And film has always taken countless forms, performed many different functions and (intentionally or not) elicited numerous effects. From the start, films have entertained, informed and educated, but also provoked, disturbed, challenged, experimented, aroused, recorded, reported, promoted, sold, persuaded and deceived.

This dizzying variety is an enduring feature of film, linking its present to its past and its future. Digital technology has transformed the ways moving images are produced, distributed and consumed, and the volume of screen 'content' has skyrocketed. But while almost none has ever seen a strip of celluloid, today's 'films' – be they features or television programmes, adverts or pop videos, gallery installations or TikToks – share a common ancestor in the first moving images to dazzle 1890s audiences.

As studios and broadcasters mine their back catalogues and public archives – who have been conscientiously preserving film heritage for many decades – open up their vaults with mass digitisation initiatives, so much that was previously largely hidden from public view is now available on a device near you. Britain has been in the vanguard of this digitisation revolution. For example, the BFI's own video-on-demand platform, BFI Player, now boasts some 15,000 films. The borders between past and present are collapsing, as are the boundaries between the mainstream and what were once assumed to be niche tastes. Silent newsreels and CGI blockbusters, Edwardian street scenes and 21st Century vlogs: all these and countless more now sit side-by-side on video streaming platforms.

This sudden superabundance demands a redrawing of the boundaries of what film in Britain is, while laying bare just how much remains unmapped. This series will strive to explore this territory, telling fresh stories, retelling and revitalising familiar ones in the light of new discoveries and shining a light on overlooked or undervalued sectors, traditions and genres of British filmmaking.

There is no more striking illustration of this than *The Story of Victorian Film* – the first single-volume account of the earliest days of filmmaking in Britain in more than 30 years. In that time, interest in early film in Britain and elsewhere has grown exponentially, thanks largely to a network of experts and enthusiasts which prominently includes this book's author.

This book is the culmination of a landmark digitisation project making the entirety of the national collection of Victorian films available for the first time. Bryony Dixon synthesises the discoveries and insights of many experts while throwing fresh light on Britain's creative and industrial contribution to an emerging medium. Crucially, she returns to the films – including many unavailable to previous generations of historians – finding new evidence of the ingenuity and innovation of Britain's fledgling filmmakers. The result is a guide that not only vividly conveys the excitement of the era and the author's own enthusiasm, but repositions Britain's role in the development of this young medium.

As the BFI's curator of silent film and an internationally respected archivist, programmer and historian – who personally oversaw the years-long project of digitisation and restoration – Bryony Dixon is uniquely qualified to guide us through this rich and often surprising territory. The story of British film starts here …

Mark Duguid & Patrick Russell

INTRODUCTION: TIME RECORDED

'Film looks like time recorded'

John B. Kuiper [1]

The emergence of any new communication media is exhilarating. Recent celebrations of 30 years of the World Wide Web took us back to its heady early days, when individuals still had an impact on what would grow to be a global phenomenon. Just as digital media changed the way we saw the world as the 20th century gave way to the 21st, so projected moving images did a century earlier. Film, then, offered a taste of the future, just as it now offers us a glimpse at the past. Like photography or the telephone, wireless telegraphy or the phonograph, film was much more than a merely tool for recording or communicating; it heralded a revolution in seeing and a paradigm shift in our relationship with the past.

The arrival of film changed the way time was recorded. Victorian film was a test bed for recording time – a great experiment in exploring the parameters of moving images. The more prescient contemporary observers saw this, among them Canadian scientist J. Miller Barr, extolling the new medium in 1897:

> A new and wonderful field in the realm of photography has lately been opened up to the world... the scientific photographers of today are enabled to portray motion in all its varied forms with a realism that impresses the beholder. The busy traffic of city streets, the play of expression upon the

human countenance, the movements of waves, waterfalls, fleeting clouds — these and many other effects have been depicted upon the screen with equal fidelity before audiences that have seldom failed to show their appreciation.[2]

That appreciation was immediate and astonishing. Word of mouth spread the news — everyone wanted to see this new world, from the monarch to the humblest child (moving pictures held a particular fascination for the young, as they still do). It took some time to penetrate all areas of society, but by the end of the Victorian era there would have been few people who hadn't seen a moving picture. But there was another, more profound impact as, Millar continues:

As a means of permanently recording and vividly illustrating notable events [film's] importance will scarcely be overestimated... I shall content myself with a brief allusion to one recent event in which the whole world has evinced keen interest — viz., the celebration of the Diamond Jubilee of Her

Queen Victoria's Diamond Jubilee (British Cinematographe, 1897).

Scenes at Balmoral (1896).

Majesty Queen Victoria. The Royal procession and other imposing features of the jubilee ceremonials were duly recorded upon cinematographic films, of which fine specimens were set aside for future preservation in England's National Museum. These have been 'hermetically sealed and deposited in the museum, together with a machine and lantern, by means of which they may be exhibited to future generations'.

We can only strive to realize, in some dim measure, the fascination which those pictured ribbons of celluloid will exercise upon the eyes and minds of future Londoners—let us say, at some remote epoch, when the throne of Great Britain will be occupied by a monarch of whom we can form no conception, under social conditions which may differ widely from those existing at the present day.[3]

We are all, as it were, Miller Barr's future Londoners, looking back through the medium of the screen at a strange but eerily familiar world, like Alice peering through the looking glass. What might we see in the Wonderland of early film?

This book is about the first six years or so of moving pictures made in Great Britain, from the time films were first projected in February 1896 to the year the Victorian age came to an end. The Queen, who had reigned for over 60 years, died early in 1901, but I have included the films for that whole year, partly because we often don't know exact production or release dates, but also because 1901, before Edward VII's coronation, is such an transitional year, in which we can see distinct signs of development in the structure of films. The book is based very largely on the evidence of the films themselves, and particularly the surviving films, which represent about 21% of the number of films that were made, according to our current knowledge. The BFI National Archive holds approximately 770 extant films from the era, of about 3,650 that we know were made, which we can use to build up a picture of what Victorian audiences were seeing.

The primary focus of the book is British films, that is, films made by a British-based filmmaker or company, even if filmed overseas. But context is also crucial; the early film business was a very international one. British–made films were exported all over Europe and America, and to many other countries across the world. Meanwhile, French and American films in particular were shown extensively in Britain. Successful films were routinely copied by other companies, so there was a constant cultural flow between the film-producing countries, which I will refer to from time to time where relevant. Contemporary sources, such as filmmakers catalogues and press, have been favoured to contextualize the films. But the Victorian era of film has been extensively written about, most notably in John Barnes' magisterial *The Beginnings of Cinema in England*, which devotes one volume to each year between 1896 and 1900. In 1989 John Fell, reviewing volume three, judged it 'the kind of history on which others draw and which is disposed to outlive its offspring.'[4] This remains true more than 30 years later, and will probably still be true 30 years hence. Barnes was absolutely confident that, as Richard Maltby observes in his introduction to the final volume,

> 'these early years were arguably the most inventive in the history of British cinema, as pioneers such as Robert Paul, George Albert Smith and James Williamson experimented with techniques of film narrative on some of the most innovative equipment in the world.'[5]

Many others have fleshed out Barnes' work on the histories of individuals, the international context and the analysis of individual films; it's a lively and burgeoning field of study. Some names will crop up throughout the book. Others can be found in the Further Reading list at the back. And recent years have seen new in-depth studies of the aforementioned pioneers, Paul,[6] Williamson and Smith.[7]

So with an abundance of historical work, do we need more? Well, yes. Our perspective has changed: the general availability of all of the surviving films, now that they have been digitised and made available online, is a revelation. Previously, apart from a handful of titles published on DVD, these were only available to view on film at the BFI, requiring in-person attendance and special equipment. There is still some identification work to do to match the images with what historians have discovered, but we no longer have to imagine what the films were like from descriptions or stills. We can also more easily compare them with surviving films from other producing countries, which substantially changes our understanding of the early film world.

Where once the researcher was forced to spend weeks, months or even years rooting through perhaps multiple archives and libraries, the past is now instantly recoverable thanks to the digitisation of millions of documents, newspapers, catalogues, books, journals and, of course, films. We now have easy access to all of the films that survive of the late Victorian era and to many of the documents that flesh out their background. It's an excellent moment to stand back and take a fresh look at the early film.

Despite plenty of fine historical writing on early film, the subject hasn't reached the mainstream of cultural knowledge, even among those studying media history. Since the middle of the 20th century, when film began to be studied seriously, early film has been seen as problematic. Partly this was a function of the difficulty of exhibiting it at that time. Beside the more familiar sound feature film, early films seemed alien: they were short, silent, filmed at differing speeds and were often available only in poor quality copies. They were studied in the context of feature films because the cinema was the principle entertainment space in which they could be projected. But if we step back from this cinema-centric view, the picture looks different. We can see that 'cinema' history is only one branch of the development of moving image. We see how, in content and style, the early films fit into a timeline of moving image forms from the late 19th century to the present, which would span magic lantern lectures and fairground sideshows, through cinema's supporting programmes up to television and online video platforms.

Theories and histories forged in the age of the feature film rarely translate well to the earlier era. One theory, however, *has* come to explain the early film and its essential differences with what followed: Tom Gunning's unifying concept of the 'cinema of attractions' neatly encompasses the very short films that were exhibited in the variety of entertainment venues present at the turn of the century – music halls, town halls and public halls and the fairgrounds. As Gunning has it, the fundamental job that these little animated photographs had to do was to convey the novelty of movement and to say 'look at me': 'This is an exhibitionist cinema'.[8]

The story of how the different types of films began to diversify from that novelty period can be told largely by looking at the films themselves and at their descriptions in contemporary catalogues. We can assess how the films went about attracting their audiences and how the dynamic interplay between producers, exhibitors and spectators began to change them. We can compare their time with our own multimedia world, in which short attractions have once again come to the fore; short videos on YouTube or TikTok often bear more than a passing resemblance to those of the Victorian era. We as audiences are still interested in many of the same things – the sensation of movement; ourselves and our neighbourhoods; distant places; personalities; news and topical events; the spectacle, the fantastic, the comic and the dramatic. But understanding the nature of the films and what they can tell us about Victorians times or Victorian people is not always straightforward.

Of all the sources for documenting recent history, early film is (alongside radio) the most neglected and misused. Poor at putting over complex ideas, infuriatingly under-documented, easy to use out of context and, in the early period, rarely showing what historians want most to support their arguments, it is too often a kind of moving wallpaper for the rehashing of simplified history in television documentaries. Yet film has an irresistible quality – it fixes in the memory in a way that words only occasionally do. It more closely approximates to our sense of reality than any other medium.

One of the first people to tackle the subject of the uses of film for the historian was the writer and theorist Barbara Deming, a film analyst at the

Library of Congress during the 1940s. Deming believed that films could do more than provide photographic evidence of events in a historical period; they could offer insights into mentality and psychology. So fiction could serve the analysing historian just as well as the more obviously evidential non-fiction films: 'it would be possible for the historian to have before him all the so-called topical films of a period and still not learn the period's chief hopes and fears.' Applying Deming's analytical approach to fictional films of the Victorian era is challenging – their short length may not reveal as much about Victorian mentality or psychology as we would like – but about one thing she was very clear:

> The historian deserves the most significant, most reliable and most vivid evidence. The evidence need be significant in no obvious or public sense. It also need not be reliable strictly on its own merits – supplementary evidence may play a role. But it needs to be vivid in specifically movie terms; the look afforded the historian should be one he could not duplicate through some other medium.[9]

Pope Leo XIII Leaving Carriage and Being Ushered into Garden (British Biograph, 1898).

Illustration of Biograph's filming of the Pope (*Scientific American*, January 14, 1899, p. 24)

That quality of vividness is certainly something that watching the films themselves can provide, but interpretation requires some help. As then *Sight and Sound* Editor Penelope Houston warned in 1967, film as evidence could be:

> untrustworthy, superficial, vulnerable to every kind of distortion; and at the same time irreplaceable, necessary, a source material that no twentieth century historian ought to disregard, though many may still seem prepared to.[10]

In the 21st century historians are still disregarding film as a source. Most recent historical works on the Victorian and Edwardian eras barely mention film, many not at all.[11] It was certainly much harder to access film in the mid-20th century than it is in the digital age. With all of the surviving films from the Victorian period now available for free, and in higher quality, thanks to a specially-funded digitisation programme at the BFI National Archive, we can only hope that the films will be included with more routinely considered documents by writers, academics and broadcasters, and not just as a period-appropriate backdrop. As Deming urges,

> The job so far has been to scan the film for its value as a direct mirror of the period. The job from here is to step through the looking glass – to seek revelations about the people who made the films and about the people for whom the films were made.[12]

Any such revelations are immeasurably enhanced by a knowledge of the key players in the birth of film in Britain and their contribution to how it developed across those first few years. Their stories are woven through the following chapters, which, I hope, capture some of the thrill that the emergence of this medium had on them.

Films in this early stage were not individual works of art, they were commercial products; novelties for a rapidly growing mass market. The men who made them were working in a heated, competitive environment. They were mostly young – in their twenties and thirties – and ambitious. Their audience, too, was young; the mean age of Britain's population in the 1890s was about 24, compared to 42 in the 2020s. The young flocked to the towns and cities in search of work creating a vibrant market for news, education and entertainment. And it was into the world of entertainment that moving images initially moved, because that was where the filmmakers could find the largest audiences and make their fortunes.

The early filmmakers – and the more astute contemporary observers like J. Miller Barr – were very aware of the revolution in our ways of seeing brought by the moving image, and were convinced of film's long term value. As early as 1896, Robert Paul, early British film's most important producer, made an attempt to establish a collection of film for preservation. John Barnes quotes this report from the *Era*, dated 17 October 1896:

> Mr R. W. Paul began his experiments in animated photography in a scientific spirit, and was, maybe, a little surprised to find himself plunged into

the vortex of professional life. He still hopes to give the animatographe a value apart from its entertaining quality, and offered the authorities of the British Museum a series of films recording events of today, which he thought would be greatly appreciated a century hence. The suggestion was received with delight by the museum authorities as a body. Then arose a question as to the particular authority concerned. The film was neither a print nor a book, nor – in fact, everybody could say what it was not; but nobody could say what it was. The scheme was not exactly pigeon-holed. The real trouble was that nobody could say to which particular pigeon-hole it belonged! [13]

In the end no pigeon-hole could be found at the Museum or Library. Probably the scale and technical complexity of the task and the associated costs put off the keepers. It would be nearly another four decades before the job of preserving film was begun, by which time Paul had burned his negatives and most of the world's earliest films were lost. What does survive, then, is all the more valuable to us. And now, at last, it is all available to see, and in considerably better quality than before.

Why is it important? Because of the growth of digital communication more of our history will be visual in the future, so we must strive to provide the vividness, which film does so well, to bring the past alive for historians and the public. To do this we need to understand the nature of the films themselves and, following Deming, the careers of 'the people who made the films' who can ultimately connect us to the 'people for whom they were made'. In the following chapters we will examine the films broadly by type, as described in the contemporary catalogues issued by producers and distributors of film and in genres that we might recognise today – from actualities and travel films, to comedies and dramas.

But we will begin at the point when films were first projected publicly in Britain – in early 1896, a few weeks after the Lumière brothers' famous Paris show – and consider why it was that film, which might have become an artefact of science, of education or even of art, became part of the world of entertainment.

Montage: Meet the Pioneers

CLOCKWISE FROM TOP LEFT:

Robert William Paul (1869-1943): a trained electrical engineer, Paul developed and sold all kinds of equipment. He began manufacturing copies of Edison's kinetoscope and made films for it with Birt Acres in 1895. He showed his first projected films in February 1896, patented and sold cameras and projectors, and opened his film studio in 1898.

George Albert Smith (1864-1959): an illusionist, actor and entertainment entrepreneur, Smith ran a pleasure park at St Anne's Well and married popular actress Laura Bayley, who he met on tour with J. D. Hunter's theatrical company. He printed films for many different film pioneers, especially Charles Urban, and went on to develop the Kinemacolor colour process.

Birt Acres (1854-1918) was a professional photographer who turned cinematographer in 1895. He was particularly interested in the photography of natural phenomena and in the educational uses of film. He worked with Paul in 1895 making films for the Kinetoscope, but when they fell out Acres pursued his own filmmaking path, filming for Stollwerck in Germany and setting up his own show in Piccadilly.

Cecil Hepworth (1874-1953): the son of a famous magic lanternist and scientific lecturer, Hepworth could turn his hand to all aspects of the young art of film; technical development, writing and directing. He worked briefly with Birt Acres and Charles Urban before setting up his own studio and lab. In 1897 he wrote *The ABC of Cinematography*, Britain's first film book.

Charles Urban (1967-1942): Urban was an entrepreneurial American, previously an encyclopaedia salesman, who came with his Bioscope projector to Britain to work for Maguire and Baucus, agents for Thomas Edison's films. He renamed the company Warwick Trading Co. building it into of the most successful early film businesses in the UK.

William Kennedy-Laurie Dickson (1860-1935): one of the top contenders in the 'who invented cinema' stakes. He will always be more associated with his pioneering work on film for Thomas Edison in the US, but he was a key figure in the film business of Victorian Britain. A scientific all-rounder from a highly cultured background, he was also a great showman who set the highest standards for the new art.

Laura Bayley (1862-1938): the most significant and influential woman in early British film, Laura Bayley was a professional actor specialising in pantomime, who acted in many of the films made by her husband, G. A. Smith. His cash book mentions her taking the Biokam 17.5mm camera out to shoot some films which were sold with the camera/projector for home use.

James Williamson (1853-1933) ran a chemist's shop in Hove with a sideline in photographic equipment. He was a keen photographer who also gave lantern entertainments, to which he added film. From 1896 he closed the chemist's to focus on making films and exhibited them on a Wrench projector.

Early film pioneers were far from the top-hatted Victorian inventors of popular legend. They came from a variety of backgrounds: some were inventors, but others brought all kinds of skills and specialised knowledge into the new profession, which would in turn leave their mark on the films they made.

Among their number were engineers, photographers, performers, exhibitors and entrepreneurs – and some pioneers had experience in several of those roles.

1. 'NOVELTY? IT'S AS OLD AS THE HILLS'[14]: FILM AND THE MUSIC HALL

The film was born into a dazzling world of late 19th century entertainments where music hall was king. Thrill-seeking Victorian punters lapped up variety acts: ribald songs and lion tamers, contortionists and barrel jumpers. Aerialists mounted death-defying stunts above their heads, magic lanternists cast beautifully coloured transformations onto large screens and phantasmagoria projected the demons of hell on clouds of oily smoke. Film, when it came, was just one more novelty in a multitude of novelties.

As with many novelties, it was in the great city centre music halls that the earliest shows were exhibited commercially. Within weeks of trade screenings to music hall managers, photographic societies and engineers in February 1896, the French Lumière Company's Cinematograph opened at the Empire Leicester Square and Robert Paul's Theatrograph opened at The Egyptian Theatre in Piccadilly, Olympia, moving soon after to the Alhambra, the Empire's rival on Leicester Square. The young engineer Robert Paul had not planned to exhibit his films as an entertainment – he was more interested in selling film apparatus – but was persuaded to turn showman to cash in on the moving picture craze.

The music hall was a natural home for the film shows. Here was a ready-made infrastructure: an exhibition space with a stage, an orchestra and an enthusiastic audience. And, crucially, here too was the means of dissemination: a loose network of theatres, a trade press, a publicity machine that fed on novelty and a kind of bush telegraph that could carry news of a novelty, a song or a joke like lightning through the pubs and schoolyards of the land.

Inside the London Music Hall, Shoreditch (1900), from G. R. Sims' *Living London Magazine*.

The West End music halls did fantastic business, with film shows playing to packed houses. Moving picture soon became the new favourite part of the variety programme, and producers and exhibitors all over the country quickly climbed on the bandwagon. The same thing was happening in early 1896 all over Europe, America and, soon, in many other countries around the world. This was principally due to the remarkably well-developed business strategy of the Lumière brothers, who had a particular genius for packaging and distributing their product worldwide. Having showcased the Cinematographe and its film show at the very end of 1895, they busied themselves through 1896 sending out operators, working as franchisees. The operators would film some local scenes, then encourage local entrepreneurs to do the same, thereby creating a market for the Lumières' equipment and an edge over their competitors. Like many early filmmakers, the Lumières expected to make their money out of this new marvel by selling hardware – cameras, projectors and processing services – rather than 'software', that is, the films themselves.

American Biograph at the Palace (British Biograph, 1899).

The first film shows were a motley collection of subjects based on scenes that were to hand, like the Lumières' *Sortie d'usine Lumière à Lyon* (*Workers Leaving the Lumière Factory*, 1895) or Birt Acres *Rough Sea at Dover* (1895). But as new films were made, increasingly with music hall audiences in mind, they began to imitate the 'turns' at the music hall. Existing attractions like the kinetoscope and magic lantern shows also provided inspiration for popular subjects. The programmes of the various 'first' projected film shows reveal a mix of subjects that exploited the special qualities of the moving picture. Most popular were those that gloried in the simple movement of natural phenomena, such as sea waves, or those that conveyed a sense of exhilaration, such as trains rushing past, busy street scenes or sport. These simple scenes were supplemented by more 'staged' offerings that chimed with the interests and taste of the music hall audience: boxing kangaroos, acrobatics, dances and comic scenes.

This kind of fare would have been familiar to viewers who had seen W. K. L. Dickson's 35mm films in a Kinetoscope parlour. While working for the Edison Company in New Jersey, Dickson's choice of subjects for the Kinetoscope included, inevitably, many vaudeville attractions from the great New York music halls, such as Keith's Union Square or Koster and Bial's. He tempted the performers to the famous 'Black Maria' studio he had constructed for Edison. A famous name was a particular asset in the Kinetoscope parlour, where the customer would choose one subject, rather than a whole programme as at the later projected show. Legendary acts such as sharpshooter Annie Oakley, strongman Eugene Sandow and dancers Ruth St Denis and Annabelle were powerful attractions. These could have been seen in London in 1894, in a parlour at 70 Oxford Street, and they inevitably set the bar for future film subjects, which aimed to capitalise on the evident popularity of great variety celebrities and the craving for novelty.

If it was an obvious step for filmmakers to film the great stage artistes of the day, there were also great pay-offs for the performer. As film shows spread outside London, audiences all over the country could see their stage favourites for a fraction of the price of attending a live theatre performance. For the performer, the benefits of publicity and exposure came without the cost of a gruelling round of stage performances – sometimes several in one night. Music hall and variety stars were filmed in some numbers: novelty dancers, acrobats, pantomime artists, quick-change men, 'lightning' artists, jugglers and thespians. By 1900, audiences could see, and even hear, the ever-popular singers who made up a large part of the bill, miming to recordings of themselves on cylinder or disc [see 'Close-up', pp. 168–9].

As the film show bedded in to the music hall programme during 1896, audience tastes began to influence the production of films. 'While the highly favoured genres tended to be actualities, and natural subjects continued to be popular, there was also a demand for comedy and story, which music hall audiences were used to. Music hall managers were particularly active in responding to their audiences, as well as in promoting their performers. Writing in 1936, Robert Paul recalled: 'In April, the Alhambra manager, Mr Moul, who wisely foresaw the need for adding interest to wonder, staged upon the roof a comic scene called *The Soldier's Courtship*, the 80-foot film of which caused great merriment.'[15] One of the first fictional story films,

R. W. Paul's *The Soldier's Courtship* (1896).

Paul's *The Soldier's Courtship* (1896) used well-known actors Fred Storey and Julie Seale – as well as Paul's wife Ellen – and borrowed props and costumes from the theatre.

It was a simple story, well told: a soldier and his girl are kissing on a park bench when a woman comes along and sits on the bench spoiling their fun. The exasperated soldier tips up the bench, throwing the woman to the ground and carries on kissing his girl. This kind of knockabout, slightly bawdy humour was well-pitched to music hall audiences' tastes, and it's no surprise that it went down well at the Alhambra.

Rooftops were a convenient spot for shooting films in large urban areas. Paul used the Alhambra's roof for several films. In New York, W. K. L. Dickson had used the roof of Keith's Union Square theatre to set up an open-air studio built on a rotating platform that could be turned to catch the light, with a rain-proof booth for the camera. Arriving in London to set up the British Mutoscope and Biograph Company, he initially had to make do with

Outside the Empire Leicester Square, in the Lumière brothers' *Entrée du cinematographe* (1896).

a ground-level site in the Adelphi Buildings, on the Thames' Embankment, but simple sets could be created and theatre backdrops borrowed to evoke an authentic live stage performance by a favourite music hall artist. This staging – which some later commentators have seen as evidence of 'primitivism'[16] – is better understood as the filmmakers reproducing the kinds of settings that Victorian audiences knew and expected.

When film arrived on the Victorian entertainment scene, the stage – whether 'legitimate' or popular – was the dominant form, and as such was what audiences aspired to. Filmmakers responded to this by providing, in their programmes, the music hall bill in miniature: a constantly changing selection of short subjects to keep audiences entertained and interested. This might consist of topical subjects, such as the opening of the Kiel canal, the Queen's Jubilee or the progress of the Boer War; humorous sketches and songs; novelty acts such as magicians, acrobats or performing animals; short dramas, popular science or scenes of distant lands. The film show, a 'turn' in itself of 10 minutes

Film in the theatre, in R. W. Paul's *The Countryman and the Cinematograph* (1901).

(later extending in duration), could provide its own version of all these genres – even, after a fashion, the traditional music hall song (see 'Close-up', pp. 168–9).

One interesting early development, the clever idea of Lumière's international operators, was to film the exterior of whichever theatre was hosting their show. In London, *Entrée du cinematographe* (1896) shows an ostensibly natural street scene outside the Empire Leicester Square, with carriages drawing up and pedestrians walking past. Posters for the Cinematographe show and for the ballet, *Faust*, can be seen on the theatre's hoarding. In fact the scene is carefully staged. Among those who just happen to be passing by are Félicien Trewey, the Lumière's operator, walking beside the manager of the Empire, Charles Dundas Slater. Also passing by are a troupe of 'blackface' minstrels – a harmful racist tradition pervasive in Victorian entertainment. This particular troupe appear in another Lumière film made the same day. As part of the show, the audience would see the exterior of the building they had just entered – a cleverly self-aware piece of marketing.

R. W. Paul's recently rediscovered *Fun on the Clothes-Line* (1896).

Fiction films, too, can give us an impression of what the Victorian film show was like. R. W. Paul's *The Countryman and the Cinematograph* (1901) shows us a theatre space with proscenium arch and roll-down screen; the orchestra would be in the pit under the front of the stage, while the boxes would be directly next to the stage. *American Biograph at the Palace* (1899), made by the British Mutoscope and Biograph Company, shows a painted backdrop of a street scene in which a bill poster is pasting up an advertisement for the 'Biograph at the Palace', the very theatre in London's Cambridge Circus where the American Biograph was resident for some years.

The term 'American', incidentally, was there to lend cachet to the show. In fact, it was entirely run by the British company and showed films by the British producers, although it was affiliated with the New York firm and would import a selection of its best films. 'American' in the context of early film denoted a robust, modern spirit of invention and novelty to which British audiences clearly responded. A. D. Thomas, an endearingly outrageous showman, even styled himself 'Edison Thomas' to derive any competitive advantage out of an entirely fictional association with the legendary inventor.

Some producers were in a stronger position to make films of music hall artists than others. Just as R. W. Paul put his Alhambra connections to good use, so W. K. L. Dickson and Walter Gibbons could call on performers from venues with which they had developed relationships. A great range of artists were captured on film, from legends of the 'legitimate' stage, such as Herbert Beerbohm Tree or Sarah Bernhardt, to popular stage celebrities, including Dan Leno and Herbert Campbell, along with famous acts of the day now largely forgotten.

In Robert Paul's recently rediscovered *Fun on the Clothes-Line* (1896), slack-wire walker Harry Lamore recreates the music hall turn which he performed for some years around the London circuit, including at the Alhambra and the Palace Theatre of Varieties. A review of the Alhambra programme on 23 February, 1895 singles out Lamore for praise as 'a quaint and original wire performer [who] evokes applause by the activity with which he springs upon the wire from the

Absurd spectacle: R. W. Paul's *The Deonzo Brothers* (1901).

stage and creates curiosity and amusement by the eccentric costume which he removes entirely while standing on the thin thread of steel.'[17] The scene resembles set-ups like G. A. Smith's *Hanging out the Clothes* (1897), with a wife discovering her husband's amorous advances on the maid on laundry day.

Another Paul film features a popular Canadian act who were touring the international music hall circuit with their intrepid barrel-jumping act. *The Deonzo Brothers* (1901) encapsulates the delights and frustrations of Victorian film. With its deliciously absurd spectacle of grown men jumping in and out of barrels for a living, it illustrates the lengths to which the search for novelty would go. The act is truly spectacular, commencing with the two men jumping from a standing start, blindfolded, into a barrel. They progress to barrels mounted higher up in a pyramid formation, climaxing with a grand finale in which both will jump out of their barrels into just one barrel at the pyramid's apex… at which point the film ends abruptly. This invariably draws a sigh of disappointment from contemporary audiences, but such is the nature of these rare survivors – it's so often the beginnings and ends of film prints that are missing. Fortunately, one great benefit of the flourishing illustrated press in this era is the chance to find references to people and events presented in the films. The popular illustrated monthly the *Harmsworth Magazine* contains a very full report of the Brothers' act, complete with illustrations showing the still blindfolded pair making it, impossibly, into the top barrel.[18]

Many film producers did not enjoy close links to any particular theatre. The Warwick Trading Company specialised in distribution from the start, acting from 1894 as agents for Edison's Kinetoscope, before switching to projected film and equipment sales. Warwick's offer was an extensive catalogue of 'topicals' (see Chapter 3), along with all the other types of film, made by their own staff and as agents for other producers. These would have been sold on to any exhibitor who wanted to include them in his show. Even so, Warwick were well connected to the central London music hall business. It was most likely Charles Urban, working for Warwick, who commissioned the film *Will Evans the Musical Eccentric* (1899), which featured this popular artiste in his mandolin-playing, tumbling act ('eccentric' here meaning acrobatic). Will Evans was music hall royalty: a comic performer in the circus and pantomime tradition, who also sang, danced and wrote plays. His father, Fred Evans, was a celebrated pantomime performer and arranger of Harlequinades, while Will's

Agoust Family of Jugglers (1898).

nephew, also Fred, would be a hugely popular silent film comedian of the 1910s, best known for his character 'Pimple'.

George Albert Smith, working on the South coast, had his own popular theatre connections, notably in the form of his wife, Laura Bayley, who performed with her sisters in pantomimes at the Brighton Aquarium. Several of Smith's films feature Bayley, acting in comedies such as *The Kiss in the Tunnel* (1899) and *Let Me Dream Again* (1900) and performing in pantomime (the pantomime films, from a production of Mother Goose, were made in 1902, just outside of the scope of this book). She also appears as the tragic crossing-sweep from Dickens' *Bleak House* in *The Death of Poor Joe* (1900).

Only a fraction of the films made during these six years survive. Among the most tragically missing are R. W. Paul's *Difficulties of an Animated Photographer* (1898), arguably the first ever film about filmmaking, and a number of films starring celebrated magicians Nevil Maskelyne and David Devant, some of which have recently been re-animated from still images in magazines or flick-book versions. A few other films of famous music hall performers exist only as Filoscope versions. The Filoscope was a flick book devised by Henry Short, who had worked with R. W. Paul and Birt Acres. Short appears in two of Britain's first films – *Incident at Clovelly Cottage* and *Cricketer Jumping over Garden Gate*, both shot in early 1895. Some films survive as series of reduced photos, reproduced for the Filoscope from film frames. These include films of the great comedian and pantomime dame Dan Leno, and the bizarre-looking George Chirgwin, whose own distinctive take on the racist blackface tradition was to complement his make-up with a white diamond over one eye, which saw him billed as 'The White-Eyed Kaffir'[19]. Some of these record micro-performances, others celebrity appearances, as with a series of films featuring Dan Leno and fellow Music Hall Society members (including the cream of music hall artistes: Leno's professional partner Herbert Campbell, Will Evans, Joe Elvin, Harry Randall and George Robey) on a "Water Rats" day out. There were other films of Leno taken at the annual Music Hall charity sports day at Herne Hill, an event first filmed by Robert Paul in *Comic Costume Race* (1896). That film does, mercifully, survive, and shows the contestants racing towards wicker costume baskets, from which they don wig, hat and fancy costumes and career back to the start. The film's popularity highlights the late Victorians' fascination with their celebrities – filmmakers continued to film the event every year. These few films that preserve for us something of the delights of the music hall and variety theatres are among the most precious to survive from this era.

The early manufacturers' catalogues are brimming with references to music hall: the place, the people and its practices. Until they diverged in the late 1900s, the film and music hall businesses were inextricably linked. But while the film show may have started in the music hall as just another novelty 'act', the elements of the show – the actualities, comedies, dramatic sketches or travel films – would in time expand, subdivide and bloom into separate film genres, each demanding its own section in the catalogues. Each genre addressed a need or desire catered for in the music hall programme: for news and information, for the delights of familiar or faraway places, for laughter, entertainment and drama; for favourite stories brought to life, for magical worlds of the imagination. A moving picture show could offer something to satisfy all of these demands, and the fledgling medium now began to develop along these genre lines.

Close-up: The Victorian Film Catalogue

To begin to understand Victorian film, we should forget everything we know about the later cinema industry. Banish thoughts of auteurs, release schedules, critics: you'll find none of these. Perhaps the best sources we have for exploring the business and culture of early film are the producers' and distributors' catalogues. It's frustrating how few exist, considering how useful they are for identifying films of the era. In many cases, photographs or descriptions of films are all that remain. Whole careers survive only in the pages of these catalogues.

Catalogues were published by different kinds of businesses. Robert Paul's sales catalogue contains his films (including some originally made for the Kinetoscope) alongside the equipment for which he was famous, as the first maker in the world to sell cine cameras. Others, like Phillip Woolf, were distributors, so listed other film-makers' product. Initially films were presented simply in list form, but as more were offered films began to be grouped by something resembling genre. Warwick's 1897/8

Warwick Trading Co. catalogue, issued in 1902.

catalogue lists: 'Humorous films', 'Reversing films', 'Spookey' (sic), 'Pantomime', 'Spectacular films', 'Magical and trick Series', 'Civic', 'Circus', 'Carnival Processions', 'Contests', 'Races and Sports', 'Ballet and Dances', 'Animal', 'Circus and Zoological', 'Street and Descriptive Scenes', 'Sea Shore Subjects', 'Marine and Aquatic', 'Railway Subjects', 'Panorama from moving Train', 'Steamer and Tram', 'Naval and Military subjects', 'South Africa General Descriptive', 'Fillis "Savage South Africa" Series', 'Gymnastics and Drill Subjects', 'Fire Series' and 'Representative Industries'.

This tells us a lot about what subjects filmmakers chose to make, what was original or influenced by other filmmakers, and what proved popular with audiences. Films might have some description or even a full synopsis, and in more expensively-produced catalogues, some would also have illustrations or photographs.

But it's not just the films that catalogues can tell us about; they can show how films were grouped together. Travel films, for example, were offered individually or in series. By the time of its 1901/2 catalogue, Walturdaw was repackaging films in sets and themed programmes of 15, 30 or even 60 minutes, including 'The Life and Death of Queen Victoria'; a children's programme; a Christmas party programme; a 'smoking concert' package; Navy and Army packages and films 'suitable for Sunday afternoons'.

The catalogues occasionally reveal who shot the films (Joe Rosenthal in South Africa and China, G. A. Smith or Charles Urban in Italy), include advice on programming (such as seasonal and children's offerings), or present feedback on what other audiences have found funny, sensational or moving. Other anecdotal comments, such as the recommended presentation of a comic scene like *The Kiss in the Tunnel* – sandwiched between two 'phantom ride' subjects – alert us to new developments in film presentation. There is no other way we could know this.

Catalogues tell us about film prices, use of colouring, types of equipment and accessories (for example, when the first swivel-headed tripod was marketed, enabling a smooth 360-degree panoramic shot). They show us the premises from which a company operated, so we can assess its status. They tell us about laboratories, printing and processing methods, and workrooms where film was inspected, cut and packaged. We can discern how many people might have been employed there, how lavish the manager's office was. There is a wealth of incidental detail. Paul's 1898 catalogue mentions advertising materials and glass title slides. The catalogue was issued in three languages (so we know he was exporting) and includes information about identifying characteristics of Paul's films (an embossed stamp and square frame). As a window into the world of Victorian film, the filmmaker's catalogue is hard to beat.

2 'TWO HUNDRED LIES A MINUTE': ACTUALITY AND NEWS

Of all the genres that developed from those earliest shows, moving pictures of 'news', that is, real events as they happened, were the most highly prized. They were rare. It's difficult enough now, with all the technology at our disposal, to capture rapidly developing situations on film; for Victorian cameramen it was nigh on impossible. Not that they didn't try. A few precious surviving examples of such films testify to the spirit of adventure and 'can do' approach of our early filmmakers.

At the end of the 19th century, the printed press was going through a period of rapid expansion, as Michael Chanan notes:

> If music hall was the dominant form of popular entertainment at the moment of the birth of film, the dominant mass medium of the day was the press. The massification of publishing in the nineteenth century came about through improvements in the means of both production and distribution: the development of rapid printing techniques using the steam press, and the advantages for distribution, both of speed and geographical dispersion, provided by the railways, of which the book publishers also took advantage.[20]

The first filmmakers were not journalists and were not, for the most part, in the business of producing 'hard news': films, after all, were exhibited in venues primarily as part of a programme of entertainment. Films a minute or so long could hardly compete with newspapers in explaining complex events or ideas, but they could illustrate and amplify stories from other news media, perhaps by showing the locations where momentous events, such as the Second Boer War, were taking place, or by presenting the people who were involved. Filmmakers who had the means to do so sent cameramen overseas, but most had to be satisfied with filming the departures of troops from British ports to the Empire's distant wars. When even that opportunity was unavailable, they imitated the picture papers by dramatising real or imagined episodes from the conflict, with local moorlands standing in for the Veldt or abandoned Sussex villas passed off as remote mission stations in China. People flocked to see these films. In the ever more visual culture of late-Victorian Britain, where illustrations trumped prose and photographs trumped illustrations, moving pictures could trump them all. From simple *reportage* to overblown tales of derring-do, the actualities and reconstructions were complementary to existing frameworks of news delivery – the papers and illustrated magazines – but they also offered a layer of sensation that other news media couldn't match.

The first piece of what we might call 'breaking news', that is, a newsworthy event in the process of happening, was filmed by chance. At least

The Launch of HMS Albion (Prestwich Manufacturing Co., 1898).

three filmmakers chose to cover the launch of the battleship *HMS Albion* from the dockyard at Blackwall on the Thames on 21 June 1898. The launch of a state-of-the-art warship was a major event, and the spectacle it offered, as well as the pride of local shipworkers and their community, drew a huge and festive crowd. But what should have been a pleasant topical item, of the kind that was bread and butter to the filmmaker of 1898, turned out very differently. The cameras were on hand to capture a tragedy, as the backwash from the launching ship sideswiped a temporary stand carrying too many spectators, knocking more than 200 people into the water and causing 38 deaths, many of them women and children. Nothing of the tragedy is present in Prestwich's film of the day: the large 60mm stock gives a magnificent view of the ship going down the slips, but the camera angle conceals the ill-fated stand. The surviving fragments of Robert Paul's film, on the other hand, show the event from the water, and in the second shot we see the small rowing boats that have been picking up survivors. If we look closely we can see the drenched suits of men who have been in the water. One of the boatmen appears to be gesticulating angrily at the camera. He may just be warning

R. W. Paul's *The Launch of HMS Albion* (1898).

them not to get too close. But the appropriateness of the camera's intrusiveness and of the subsequent exhibition of the film would soon be called into question.

The filmmakers themselves were divided on the issue. A few days after the tragedy, Birt Acres, whose own film of the event doesn't survive, lambasted his rivals in a letter to the *Daily Chronicle*:

> it having come to my knowledge that someone had taken an animated photograph of the poor sufferers struggling in the water, I wish to disassociate myself in the most emphatic manner from the producers of these photographs.[21]

Acres somewhat undermined his claim on the moral high ground by offering to supply his own films for fundraising events. Even so, it must have been a stinging challenge for his one-time business partner, Robert Paul. For his part, Paul felt his decision to release his film of the tragedy was justified to raise money for the disaster fund. In his reply on 27 June, he was at pains to stress his crew's contribution to the rescue effort:

> [our boat] immediately went up and assisted twenty-five of the submerged persons on board and took them to the dock head. The camera continued photographing, but no consideration of the result was allowed to interfere with the work of rescue... I offered gratuitous exhibition at a benefit performance at the Paragon E., a collection to be made for the sufferers.[22]

To make matters worse, another (anonymous) contributor complained that the films were being shown at the Royal Music Hall in Holborn on 22 June without any such collection having been made: 'Surely so grave an insult to the best feelings of mankind ought not to pass unreprimanded.'[23] According to contemporary press reports, however, this show (given by A. D. Thomas, who had apparently bought what sounds like a copy of Paul's film) was at least distinguished by the audience baring their heads as the orchestra played the hymn 'Rocked in the Cradle of the Deep'. But all in all, it's hard to say that any of the filmmakers covered themselves in glory over this incident, as issues of taste in what moving pictures could show came under discussion for the first time. The new medium clearly had work to do to earn public trust.

Queen Victoria's Diamond Jubilee (Prestwich Manufacturing Co., 1897), near Parliament Square.

Less controversial were the actuality films of the great state occasion of the age, Queen Victoria's Diamond Jubilee, a public spectacle that would attract nearly all of the world's filmmakers active in June 1897 (Thomas Edison was the only film producer of standing not to cover the event). Some 40 cameramen, sent by over 20 companies, were positioned along the route, each attempting to get the best pictures he could of the Queen's carriage and troops representing all the nations of the Empire. The prize, if he succeeded, was potentially undreamt-of sales and a massive international audience.

The public part of the event, masterminded by Joseph Chamberlain, then Secretary of State for the Colonies, was not the usual procession of royals with their personal military guards but an unprecedented assembly of military representatives from across the Empire. Troops from six continents processed through London in splendid uniforms, making a pleasingly varied show for the three-million-strong crowd who lined the streets, leaning from every window and balcony in anticipation of a glimpse of the Queen.

The 11 surviving films (multiple duplications of which have left us with a baffling array of copies) show a good deal of the procession, which wound its way from Buckingham Palace through the city, pausing at St Paul's, then heading over the river through Borough and back over Westminster Bridge before returning to the Palace. Rival cameramen battled to secure a good vantage point. Arguments and even lawsuits ensued when those renting out space in the stands erected at points along the route interfered with a cameraman's view. Some, like Robert Paul, had more than one cameraman to maximise their chances of getting the most valuable pictures of all – those featuring the Queen herself.

What the cameras couldn't capture, of course, was the sound: of the many military bands lining the route and the many more regimental marching bands, all of which were surpassed, according to contemporary reports, by the cheering at the arrival of the Queen's carriage, a huge roar that moved like a wave as she passed. But the films offer their own visual representation of this in the frantic flapping of white handkerchiefs at the sight of the open carriage, recognisable to all by its eight cream-coloured horses in elaborately decorated harness. The 78-year-old queen, attended by her daughter-in-law, Alexandra, Princess of Wales, and her third daughter, Helena, Princess Christian, is always frustratingly hard to see – either too distant or hidden by a parasol (she suffered in old age from an eye condition aggravated by sunlight). Paul got good shots of the carriage in St Paul's churchyard, but the best surviving shot of the Queen is a fragment of a few seconds, probably taken by Alfred Wrench, showing the carriage in King William Street, just before the route goes over London Bridge.

Other Jubilee news photo opportunities survive. One film, taken by the Velograph Company, shows the Queen arriving at the garden party after the procession, while a tiny fragment, just a few frames long, survives of a film taken by W. K. L. Dickson of members of the royal family in the garden at Clarence House in July 1897. Films of the Naval Review at Spithead do not survive, except perhaps an intriguing remnant of a Biograph film of British warships at sea, called *Four Warships in Rough Seas* (c.1900), which might be from that event.

The Jubilee provides us with a snapshot of the international film industry as it stood little more than a year after the first successful public projections,

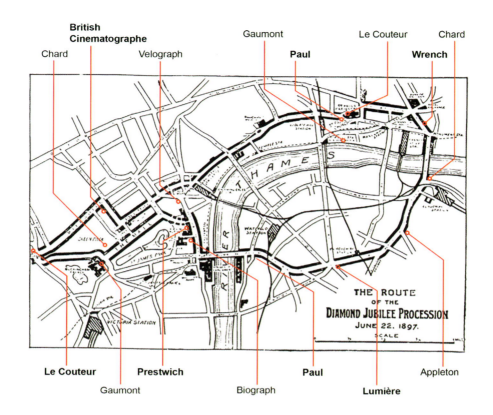

The route of Queen Victoria's Diamond Jubilee procession, showing positions of cameramen. Where at least some footage survives, the producers' names are in bold.

confidently investing in film stock and licenses for filming positions in the certain knowledge that there was a ready market for coverage of such a great national occasion – just as there has been ever since. It's difficult to attribute the surviving films, most of which are held in the BFI National Archive, to their individual filmmakers – many are fragmentary and have little or no provenance. Historians such as John Barnes and Luke McKernan have done painstaking work to identify the positions of the cameramen from press reports and memoirs.[24] More recently, access to a huge variety of digitised documents, paintings, photographs, newspapers, journals and archival collections mean that we can now reconstruct this momentous spectacle incorporating the new medium of film, and recapture some of the atmosphere of the occasion.

It's impossible to calculate how many people in Britain or round the world saw the Jubilee on film. As a national film event, it was probably unsurpassed at home until the showing of *The Battle of the Somme* in 1916. The initial popularity of the moving pictures had dipped by 1897, due to a dearth of new content and uneven presentation – flicker and unsteadiness were particular problems – and the Jubilee presented filmmakers with an unparalleled opportunity to reignite audience enthusiasm. Exhibitors showed the various series of films in any suitable venue, from the largest variety theatres to the smallest village hall, all over the country. One filmmaker, R. J. Appleton, managed 'by an amazing feat of organisation' to get his films of the Jubilee procession up to Bradford for screening on the evening of Jubilee Day, with thousands cramming into Foster Square to witness the spectacle.

The challenges of filming such a huge event would have a lasting impact on the development of film as a medium. With such a lengthy procession, filmmakers had to find ways of attaching longer reels to their cameras,

Queen Victoria's Last Visit to Ireland (1900).

which in turn made possible longer and more complex films than the simple one-shot views of 1896. The elevated shot, too, can arguably trace its origins to the Jubilee films. The whole episode gave much-needed encouragement to producers and showmen to improve the quality of their offering and to invest in the regular supply of new films. The reward was to see film acknowledged, perhaps for the first time, as a medium not just of novelty and entertainment but of historical record. As a writer in *The Era* put it:

> We owe much to the recent development of scientific photography; and by the invention of the cinematographe a means has been discovered for the preservation of what is to all intents and purposes living representations of memorable events. Our descendants will be able to learn how the completion of the sixtieth year of Queen Victoria's reign was celebrated in the capital of the country… bearing in mind the difficulties necessarily attendant upon such an undertaking, the pictures are for the most part surprisingly clear and distinct.[25]

From here on in, all public state occasions were covered by the film companies – including, naturally, Queen Victoria's funeral. By 1901 it was unthinkable that moving pictures would not be taken of the events, and like those of the Jubilee, the funeral films were distributed worldwide. Increasingly, cameras were present to document the movements of important personalities and major international events, and increasingly those personalities were aware of and, to an extent, accommodating to them. It becomes clear from the funeral footage (for example, *Funeral of Queen Victoria, Procession Starting from Victoria Station*) that Edward VII was, unlike his late mother, at pains to assist the filmmakers, even to the point of pausing the procession to allow good pictures to be taken.

These highly planned, large-scale public events at the heart of the Empire gave film companies time to prepare and secure a good vantage point, and the returns seem to have been healthy. Cameramen off to film Britain's imperial conflicts had a more challenging task. They would have to be adaptable to whatever opportunities came their way. It was expensive to send a camera team out to the Empire's constant wars. Only the well-established companies could afford the investment in travel and equipment to film somewhere like South Africa. One aspiring dabbler, the then war correspondent Winston Churchill, considered investing a half-share of £700 to take films of the Boer War, but was soon disabused of any notion that this was an enterprise for opportunists by veteran W. K. L. Dickson, who was also travelling to South Africa on the *Dunottar Castle*.[26]

But for those who couldn't make this considerable investment there were other ways to cash in on the demand for news of major international endeavours. These fitted into pre-existing show formats, from lantern lectures to more elaborate theatrical spectacles. In addition to the staged 'stories' from the Boer War there were actuality films, shot at home, of the celebrity generals – Sir Redvers Buller, Lord Roberts and the austere Kitchener – and a host of films showing troops departing and embarking on ships. Films such as the *Gordon Highlanders Leaving for the Boer War* (1899) showed the eagerness of the crowds waving them off. Almost every departing troop ship was filmed. We even see W. K. L. Dickson caught by the Warwick Trading Company camera boarding his ship in *General Buller Embarking on the Dunottar Castle* (1899).

Funeral of Queen Victoria, Marble Arch (Hepworth & Co., 1901).

Gordon Highlanders Leaving for Boer War (1899).

The films that came back from South Africa were received with huge enthusiasm, but it's difficult to determine how much of this was due to a desire for hard news, 'local colour' or patriotic stories. Many audience members would have had relatives in the army and the colonies; for the rest, the war was bound up with national pride. Having ramped up the Imperial project during the Diamond Jubilee celebrations in 1897, the establishment, including the press, now pushed the patriotic line with vigour, and the films, real or reconstructed, followed that line. The serious filmmakers who, like Dickson, actually went to South Africa in search of hard news, showed what they were permitted to – generally carefully 'neutral' or even choreographed scenes of efficient troop movements, flags being raised or heroic ambulance corps coping with difficult terrain.

No filmmaker stepped out of line and questioned the official policy, or tried to film anything the authorities didn't want them to. Most, like

Dickson and his assistants William Cox and Jonathan Seward, were in effect 'embedded', with restricted access to controversial material even if they weren't already inclined to self-censorship. The technical difficulties, especially with equipment as massive as the Biograph camera, wouldn't allow much opportunistic filming, although Joe Rosenthal, in South Africa for the Warwick Trading Company with a much more portable camera, did apparently have some of his film confiscated.

Consequently the footage being sent back from the front had limited value as 'hard' news, and yet people scrambled to see it and exhibitors continued to show it for months afterwards. So clearly there was some value specific to the moving image that people considered an important part of the mixed media that made up the 'news'. Stills photographers engaged to a greater extent in gathering contentious or graphic material. The Boer press had published images of British dead after the Battle of Spion Kop which were re-published in British journals such as the *Black and White Budget*. At least one anonymous photographer even captured images of women and children in British concentration camps. But several decades would pass before film ventured into investigative journalism. For the moment, filmmakers were in the business of appealing to the greatest possible number of viewers, not battling with the military establishment, and so took a safe, uncontroversial stance. The filmmakers came home after Ladysmith and Mafeking were relieved and Lord Roberts had raised the royal flag at Pretoria on 5 June 1900. The ceremony was captured by Rosenthal for Warwick in *Lord Roberts Hoisting the Union Flag at Pretoria*, after which he left immediately in pursuit of news in China.

As a news story, the 'Boxer Rebellion', or Yihetuan movement, was even more unreachable for the filmmaker. This uprising against official Qing toleration of foreign intervention in China (with Christian missionaries a particular target) made it very dangerous for Westerners, and this time there was no British army to travel with. Rosenthal arrived too late to film any real conflict in China but was able to capture what we might call 'local colour' in 'Pekin' (Beijing), Shanghai, Tientsin, Port Arthur, Taku and Hong Kong – the very spectacular *Ride on the Peak Tramway* (1900) survives, as does *Nankin Road, Shanghai* from the same year. The only other British survivals are staged 'stories' such as Williamson's *Attack on a Mission Station*

Unidentified film known as *Beheading a Chinese Boxer* (1900).

(1900), filmed in a disused villa near Brighton, and *Beheading a Chinese Boxer* (1900), which if genuine would be extremely gruesome – the film enacts the proceedings with an effective bit of substitution – leading us to infer that audiences were quite aware that this was a recreation. Reconstruction was a perfectly normal, and generally uncontroversial way of embellishing news stories in the entertainment repertoire.

Today's audiences, used to a vast news-gathering network of journalists, might be surprised at the apparent lack of seriousness about subjects as grave as war in early films. But the exhibition environment – the music hall or the fairground show – was not the place for sober contemplation of the facts. There were well-developed lecture circuits that catered for this, but the majority of Boer War shows were entertainments, with patriotic songs and recitations, solidly based on the premise that, as a nation, Britain had emerged victorious.

In the pages of *The Photogram*, one contemporary cynic cheerfully welcomed the new medium of film into the company of propaganda-producing agencies.

> Their Khaki-covered camera is the latest thing,
> As a fabrication mill it is the latest thing,
> Two hundred lies a minute! Why Kruger isn't in it
> With this quite unanswerable film-beats-latest thing. [27]

Genuine engagement with the real politics – the appalling nature of the war, with its concentration camps, 'scorched earth' policy, and shocking civilian death toll; the fact that Britain was *not* winning and had sacrificed a good deal of its moral authority – was never likely to be acknowledged in the environment of the music hall or fairground. When memories of the early highs and lows of the war receded and the long slog of 'winning' the war began, the patriotic shows rapidly faded away – audiences stopped coming to all but the Biograph films at the Palace Theatre, where they came more pensively 'for information'.[28]

Close-up: Black Victorians

The late-Victorian population was certainly more diverse than the surviving films would suggest. With the exception of 'local films', the cameras rarely ventured into poorer areas where immigrants tended to settle. But if we scour the films, we can find some surviving evidence of Britain's Black Victorians..

Given Britain's status as a major colonial and naval power, it's no surprise to see Black troops from African and Caribbean countries among the marchers at 'State' parades such as the Diamond Jubilee, or to find many races represented at naval parades, as in *Trafalgar Day in Liverpool* (1901). But for evidence of Britain's own Black population, we have to look hard. We find some in the films of Mitchell and Kenyon: one Black man features quite prominently in *Darwen Factory Gate* (1901), while a very young Black girl is briefly visible in a crowd of children in *Employees Leaving Brown's Atlas Works, Sheffield* (1901).

Three other examples are curiously connected. In 1899 the British Mutoscope and Biograph Company filmed *The Landing of Savage South Africa at Southampton*, heralding a troupe of South African performers in England for a spectacular arena show by circus proprietor and stunt horse rider Frank E. Fillis. Made for the 'Greater Britain' exhibition at Earl's Court, Savage South Africa (inspired by the very popular Buffalo Bill's Wild West Show) caused some controversy, much of it overtly racist (there were concerns about the moral risk to white women fascinated by the Black African men). A few commentators challenged the ethics of the enterprise; the *Times* queried 'the action of the organizers in bringing over a large number of natives to be stared at and to take their chance of being demoralized in such strange and unedifying surroundings'. Similar questions were asked in Parliament.

The show itself featured dazzling feats of horse riding and shooting and recreated battle scenes from the Matabele wars against the warriors of King Lobengula, in what became Rhodesia. The Warwick Trading Company filmed a series of scenes based on the show; only one scene survives: *Savage South Africa: Attack and Repulse* (1899). The series included the set piece Wilson's Last Stand evoking Custer, in which a gallant British Major (played by Fillis himself) fights to the death for Queen and Country against the 'savage', played by Peter Lobengula, who claimed to be the son of the defeated King. This handsome

Mitchell and Kenyon's *Miners Leaving Pendlebury Colliery* (1901).

Black performer became something of a *cause célèbre* when he attempted to marry a white woman, Kitty Jewel.

The couple's tumultuous relationship saw them in and out of the courts, through which we can trace Peter's downward spiral into poverty. He was a performer for a year of two in Manchester pantomime and eventually married an Irish woman, with whom he had four children. For a while he was a coal miner at Agecroft, near Pendlebury, Lancashire. His death in 1913, aged 38, from an aggravated form of tuberculosis may have been have been related to this. It's very tempting to connect him with the Black man seen 'play-fighting' with one of the Showman's men in the Mitchell and Kenyon film *Miners Leaving Pendlebury Colliery* (1901); the coincidence seems so strong. But the film is enigmatic. Is the Black man a miner? Is he working with the showman making the film (showmen frequently staged such 'fights' to inject some action)? We'll never know. We do know that several 'coloured gentlemen' attended Peter Lobengula's funeral, so it could be there was a larger community of Black miners or maybe these were fellow performers from the entertainment world.

3 HERE AND NOW: TOPICALS AND STREET LIFE

W. K. L. Dickson's film of the Grand National at Aintree on 24 March 1899 had a journey to the screen just as thrilling as its subject. Dickson went to extreme lengths to beat the clock, co-opting police, begging the jockeys to start the race on time when a 20-minute delay was threatened, and hiring the fastest horse in Liverpool to race to the train station (an enthusiastic crowd laid wagers on the time of arrival). From there, he travelled to London in a carriage specially converted for use as an improvised lab, complete with developing tanks and dryers, arriving at London's Palace Theatre with a finished print just in time for an 11.10pm screening. His trouble was well worth it: it was a profitable night at the Palace. Those in the audience who didn't attend the day's racing could enjoy the occasion vicariously on film, while any who had been to Aintree had the pleasure of reliving the experience – probably with a better view of the finish – and all would have benefited from seeing it in company.

The devil-may-care exuberance of early filmmakers in a new, unregulated business jumps off the pages of contemporary reporting, particularly with regard to 'topicals' – that is, films that were of the moment but not momentous. Dickson's film itself is sadly lost, but its story is one of many in the press about filmmakers getting their film to the screen in record time. The first came as early as 1896, when *The Strand* breathlessly related the tale of Robert Paul's film of the Derby on 3 June (which does survive):

> the same evening an enormous audience at the Alhambra Theatre witnessed the Prince's Derby all to themselves amidst wild enthusiasm,

(c) Drying Compartment.   Dark Room, with Developing Tank and Reel.
THE SPECIAL RAILWAY CAR.

(a)   CLEARING THE WAY FOR THE BIOGRAPH AFTER THE RACE.

W. K. L. Dickson's filming of the Grand National: illustrations in *The Golden Penny*, 1899.

which all but drowned the strains of 'God Bless the Prince of Wales', as played by the splendid orchestra... In short, the great race, as depicted by Mr Paul's Animatographe, is a veritable marvel of modern photography and mechanism.[29]

The coverage of the great social and sporting fixtures demonstrates the fierce competition between the film companies for the most lucrative footage, as well as the huge publicity that needed to be generated for a film that would very quickly become out of date. Most popular were the Epsom Derby, the Grand National, the University Boat Race, the Henley Regatta and major football and cricket matches. Securing an exclusive contract to film an event was key. The Warwick Trading Company managed to negotiate such a deal with Crystal Palace to film the FA Cup final between Sheffield United and Derby County on 15 April 1899, with the results hailed in *The Photogram* as 'half-a-dozen very fine films … [which] we believe, are the first thoroughly successful football films that have so far been produced.'[30] We don't have these particular films to judge, but others from this era that do survive tend to follow similar patterns, beginning with the arrival of the teams on the pitch (a convention still used today) and filming the play from behind the goals. With limited scope for camera movement, unresponsive film stock and lenses that made following the action next to impossible, this was the best that could be achieved.

Sport is well documented in the contemporary press, allowing us invaluable opportunities to add context to the filmed images of events. Identification of some of these films has only been possible by careful comparison with newspaper reports and photographs. Clearly, a one-minute film of a football match can tell us little about the play, but a film of similar length might capture a Derby winner in the final furlong or allow us to observe the playing style of a cricketing legend such as Prince Ranjitsinhji or WG Grace. As a document of social history, from a time when sport was just emerging as a truly mass entertainment (witness the size of the crowd in, for example, Mitchell and Kenyon's *Liverpool v Small Heath* (1901)), such films can powerfully evoke the almost religious fervour of the Victorian crowd.

As well as reports in the press, there was a rich tradition of visual representation of these annual events in painting and illustration. William Powell Frith's narrative painting 'Derby Day' (1856–58) is probably the best known of these, but at least as significant are Gustave Doré's extraordinary engravings, published in 1872 as 'London, a Pilgrimage'. Doré took all the great sporting fixtures as his subjects, particularly the great 'Londoners' day out' of the Derby, and his dawn-to-dusk structure would be emulated in later film treatments. His images transmit the exuberance of the Oxford versus

Birt Acres filming the 1895 Derby

Cambridge boat race, with its huge crowds lining the banks and hanging in festoons from the bridges of the Thames. In the only surviving fragment of film of the race from the Victorian era (sadly in a very deteriorated condition), we can just see policemen trying hard to hold back the throng as the rowers make their way down to the water. Views and scenes in early films frequently resemble the composition of well-known paintings and illustrations, and were often taken from similarly tried-and-trusted vantage points. These annual fixtures also present an unusual continuity between the lives of our Victorian forbears and our own. Following Birt Acres' film of the 1895 Derby, made for Paul's Kinetoscope, the event would be filmed every year, following the angles and echoing the aesthetic of Doré's illustrations, and likewise showing something of the mix of social classes among the spectators.

Mitchell and Kenyon's *Liverpool v Small Heath* (1901).

There was inevitably a degree of crossover between topicals, such as these sporting fixtures, and the 'news' film. The Diamond Jubilee films, for instance, might in theory straddle the two, but in practice the worldwide press attention that the event attracted positioned them firmly as news films. Likewise the 1898 funeral of four-time Liberal prime minister William Gladstone and, especially, the funeral of Queen Victoria herself three years later were undeniably major news events, but more routine royal occasions, like the Queen's 1899 visit to the Victoria and Albert Museum, belong more to the topicals category. The early catalogues of film producers also contain a bewildering array of actualities that are by no means 'news' and are less topical. These have a timeless and more general focus. Interesting and picturesque views were intended to be enjoyed for their charm and general public interest and didn't date so quickly. These might be sights to be seen in the street, such as passing traffic, children dancing to a barrel organ, fire brigade turn-outs, or other outdoor scenes such as trains entering stations, beach scenes, lifeboat launches, games on board ships, children snowballing, and opportunistically filmed events like the outdoor theatrical spectaculars at Crystal Palace or the launch of a new electric tramway.

To the modern viewer these subjects can appear a little arbitrary, defying the neat genre categorisations that we know from later cinema and television. In the very earliest days filmmakers would film any potentially appealing subject that was to hand – Louis Lumière filmed his baby daughter having her dinner or his workers leaving the factory, while Birt Acres filmed waves crashing on Dover's Admiralty pier. It was only when they could assess the reaction to particular subjects in the first film shows that filmmakers began to make more deliberate choices. Those subjects that worked well with audiences would in turn also be copied by other filmmakers.

The sheer volume of what now looks like naked plagiarism among early filmmakers is striking. Sometimes this took the form of straightforward 'duping', or duplicating a film print to make further copies – what we might call piracy (see 'Close-up' pp. 80–1) – but there were also numerous examples of almost identical restaging, or remakes. The Lumières' *Danseuses des rues*

Charles Goodwin Norton's *Children Dancing to a Barrel Organ* (1896).

Cecil Hepworth's *Arrival of Train-load of Visitors at Henley Station* (1899).

(1896) was copied by Charles Goodwin Norton as *Children Dancing to a Barrel Organ* (1898), while their *L'Arroseur Arrosé* (1895) was remade at least ten times by filmmakers including Britain's G. A. Smith and the Riley Brothers. Some apparently 'copied' films were really reproducing a broader idea, like trains pulling into stations or waves breaking on rocky shores. Birt Acres' *Rough Sea at Dover*, which he filmed for the Paul Kinetoscope in 1895, and projected for the first time at the Royal Photographic Society in January 1896, somehow found its way to New York the following April to be shown as part of the Armat Edison Vitascope show. It was so popular that the audience, quite understandably assuming that Thomas Edison had made the film himself, chanted 'Edison, Edison, speech, speech!' It was projected by Edwin S. Porter, who would go on to make many copies and remakes of British and European films under instructions from Edison's manager, William Gilmore. Shortly after, Edison's cameraman, James White, shot *Surf at Long Branch* (1896), featuring heavy surf dashing along a pier in exact imitation of Acres' film.

Charles Goodwin Norton's *A Game of Snowballing* (1898).

Accustomed as we are today to thinking about films as works of creative originality protected by copyright law, it's easy to misunderstand the reasons why producers emulated each other's films so closely. The fact is that early filmmakers were still uncertain whether moving pictures were a short-lived novelty or something that would develop. Initially, most were fixated on hardware: the marketable product was the ability of the camera, the projector and the exhibitor to deliver the show. A filmmaker would hope to patent his device and then levy a licence fee for its use or manufacture, and perhaps also to sell equipment to others and supply a range of ancillary goods and services. The patent might be a barrier to entry for potential competitors. The films themselves, on the other hand, had to attract clientele, and imitating an already successful subject was a sure way to achieve this. The films also had to display the virtues of the filmmaker's equipment and provide the means for him to display his showmanship – with no intertitles printed up for the film, audiences relied on the showman or exhibitor to provide some kind of

Launch of the Worthing LIfeboat (Biograph, 1898).

commentary, just as they did with the magic lantern show. So, in the first years, filmmakers cheerfully copied any film that looked like it was doing well with audiences. A successful subject, such as children snowballing or a fire brigade turning out, could be remade for each particular projection system.

But the risk of this routine copying, as in any market that becomes flooded with broadly imitative material, was waning consumer interest and diminishing returns. Filmmaker Cecil Hepworth complained around this time of 'interminable street scenes of which there are so many about'.[31] He wasn't alone: similar concerns seem to have led to a step change in attitudes, and to conscious efforts to broaden the repertoire and improve the technical quality of films, as *The Photogram* set out in March 1897:

> As the novelty of the subject wears away, it will be necessary to replace many of the films which audiences are now willing to tolerate, with new pictures having distinct value, either (a) for great technical or pictorial merit, or (b) for

the interest of the subject. A popular Derby day is sure to have an enthusiastic run, even if short, and good views of the coming jubilee will have a longer period of appreciation; but a good deal of the future of kinetography would seem to lie in the hands of those who will make up their own subjects for the pictures.[32]

In their pursuit of greater variety, some of the subjects filmmakers settled on – traffic in the street, people walking over bridges, countless steamers and trams and horse-drawn vehicles arriving and departing – might seem banal to us, little more attention grabbing than the output of a street surveillance camera today. But seen through Victorian eyes, even the simplest scenes held unique attractions. Traffic such as that in *Blackfriars Bridge* (R. W. Paul, 1896) communicated the sheer density of London while realistically capturing a pleasing amount of movement; a couple of years later, *Street Scene in Boar Lane, Leeds* (Riley Brothers, 1898) likely impressed viewers with the vibrancy of the city's trade, projecting an economic success story. *Arrival of Train-load of Visitors at Henley Station* (Hepworth, 1899), which shows the bourgeois British turned out in their finery for the Henley Regatta, perhaps reinforced a vision of England that filmmakers and exhibitors were keen to promote. These films attracted audiences in diverse ways, sometimes with their familiarity – their recognition factor – and at other times with their intriguing unfamiliarity. Some were even usefully instructive – suggesting what one might wear to the Henley regatta or what to expect of a busy city like Leeds.

The films of these years were resolutely upbeat. Audiences were never likely to see anything unpleasant or controversial since, to be successful, films had to be shown in an entertainment context – the music hall, the fairground or the local hall. Even the humblest street scene would have been carefully set up, with a great deal of organisation needed, as well as luck with lighting conditions: always a major factor in the success of Victorian filming given the insensitive film stocks of the time.

Other topicals may have been more local in subject, but we can infer from their prevalence in the catalogues that audiences elsewhere appreciated them nonetheless. Boat launches were a particular favourite. Among the best such films were those made on 6th April 1898 by the British Mutoscope and Biograph Company and collected under the heading *Launch of the Worthing Lifeboat*. They feature several different views showing the new lifeboat, paid for

Me and My Two Friends (Biograph, 1898).

by public subscription, being pulled by horses from its station through crowds of enthusiastic spectators. A tiny fragment survives of a scene called *Me and My Two Friends*, showing a little girl seated in the bows of the boat with a cat and the lifeboat dog, Monarch. This makes a very sweet and, to us, almost stereotypically Victorian picture. The most dramatic film shows the lifeboat coming ashore after the actual launch (the one part of the action that doesn't survive in this series). The camera is set up looking along the beach, with a striking long perspective allowing for an impressive depth of field, divided laterally by the groynes stretching to the horizon. This eye for picturesque composition – characteristic of Victorian photography – is a feature of many early actualities and travel films. Ship launches similarly appealed to filmmakers for their spectacle and natural drama, and for the crowds that they drew.

Fire brigade turn-outs, with their race-against–time momentum, had even greater dramatic appeal. These demonstrations of local crews' courage and preparedness were evidently already a popular street spectacle, thanks to the theatre of the speeding horse-drawn engines and carts. Many examples survive in the film record, and the form tends to become embellished over time: the earliest manifestations – locally identified and typically showing only the engines exiting the station – give way to more elaborate presentations, such as *Drill of the Kansas City Fire Department* (1899). This was effectively a fully-fledged show, with a particularly prestigious crew that, while in Paris for an international competition, was booked for a run at the Crystal Palace. These films show how the firemen conducted daring rescues, trained horses to jump through burning hoops and raced to reach the blaze. With all the energy, drama and emotion of speeding fire engines and intrepid rescues, it's perhaps unsurprising that these types of actuality would be the first to be narrativised, in one of Britain's most celebrated Victorian films, James Williamson's *Fire!* (1901), to which we will return.

Drill of the Kansas City Fire Dept (Warwick Trading Co., 1899).

Close-up: How to Identify Victorian Film

Very early films can be hard to identify. Victorian films were shot on short lengths of film and projected just as they were. There were no opportunities to add titles and in early shows it wasn't necessary: the filmmaker or a showman would tell audiences what they were looking at. Later, titles, made on glass magic lantern slides, were projected on a separate device to announce each film. The first known British films with titles are G. A. Smith's *Santa Claus* (1898) and R. W. Paul's *Scrooge* (1901), but with beginnings of films often missing, there may have been others.

Often, then, we must look for other evidence to distinguish between films. We may find this in the documentary record (see 'Close-up', pp. 110–11) or through observation of the film itself. Forensic examination of the film material can tell us a lot, provided the film is an original element made at the time of its release (though even later copies can tell us something). Harold Brown, the diligent former head of preservation at the BFI, pioneered a method of identification for early film. Here are a few clues to look out for:

Format: 35mm was the most common, inherited from Edison's Kinetoscope (developed by W. K. L. Dickson) and manufactured by the Blair and Eastman companies. Other companies had their own variants: from larger formats such as the British Mutoscope and Biograph Company's 68mm or the 60mm films issued by Prestwich or Gaumont, to the 17.5mm stock made for the Biokam machine. Few such odd formats outlived the Victorian era.

Perforation: Early filmmakers perforated film for their own projectors, so the shape and size of perforations on the film strip can point to a particular producer or period.

Frame lines: The shape of the camera frame and markings on the film may indicate the type of camera used.

Processing flaws: R. W. Paul's early prints were prone to discolouration, while projection wear left distinctive rectangular marks on Biograph prints. Such useful dating evidence as film stock codes and producers' logos only emerge later.

CLOCKWISE FROM TOP LEFT:

The clue is in the title: *Haggar's Bioscope Camera* (c. 1900); *Santa Claus* (1898), maybe the first printed-in title; *W. G. Grace Filoscope Film* (c. 1899), from a half-toned flip book by Henry Short, probably from an R. W. Paul film; *The Bathers* (1900) has Hepworth's round-cornered frame and concave-cut negative end; R. W. Paul's square-edged frame shape in *Children in the Nursery* (1898); still a mystery: the round perforations of *Woman Undressing* (c. 1896) could be by German Max Skladonowsky or Briton Esmé Collings; *Launch of the Oceanic* (British Biograph, 1898) bears telltale rectangular abrasion marks, made by the projector transport; Warwick Trading Company's arrow-style logo stamped on to a frame of *Trip to Vesuvius* (1901); the same logo embossed on the film leader.

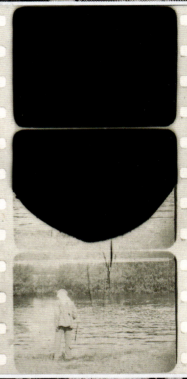

4 EVERYBODY MARCHES: MILITARY FILMS

With a massive Empire to police, the military were very visible in late-Victorian British society. Troops appeared in military spectacles such as the army reviews at Aldershot and the great Naval reviews at Spithead off Portsmouth, at celebrations like Trafalgar Day, on every state occasion and in *reportage* from war. The Queen, as Commander-in-Chief of the armed forces, warranted military attendance at most royal events, outshining the political leadership in terms of photographable pageantry. If the films from this era were our only historical source, we could be forgiven for thinking that the monarch was considerably more powerful than she was in reality.

The six-year period of Victorian film coincided with three major imperial conflicts that would influence both the development of the medium and the reporting of war. For the first time, film cameramen took their cameras to the theatre of war. The Sudan campaign, ending in 1899, was filmed by John Benett Stanford (although no film survives), while the Second Boer War, beginning the same year, was extensively covered by several cameramen. No cameraman could reach China quickly enough to film the 'Boxer Rebellion' of 1900, but there were several film reconstructions and some contextual films by Joe Rosenthal and others. The increase in military activity gave it an immediacy and a gravity that filmmakers were keen to exploit. The celebrity generals and admirals were recorded embarking on ships and returning from famous victories, while whole series of films were dedicated to the daily routines of ordinary soldiers and sailors.

An astonishing number of the films produced in Britain in the Victorian period were on military subjects. These averaged 32% of all films known to have been produced between 1895 and 1901, but this figure conceals far higher numbers for individual years: 38% in 1897, the year of the Jubilee, and an astonishing 54% in 1900, at the height of the Boer War. 8% of Mitchell and Kenyon's films over the same period were military-related.[33]

And the military manner extended further than just the troops; from orphans to religious societies to professional organisations, everybody marched. With their banners and flags, uniforms and musicians, parades and processions were a form of social expression, conveying the sense of a well-organised, unified society. For early filmmakers; these events offered spectacle and constant movement before the camera, while the marchers themselves might later be persuaded to pay to see themselves on screen. For every military cadet or bandsman parading, there were perhaps a dozen proud relatives who could be tempted into a theatre.

Birt Acres' *Charge of the 12th Lancers* (1897).

Four Warships in Rough Seas (Biograph, c. 1897).

The popularity of the military allowed filmmakers scope to present films to the public in a variety of forms. The Boer War films in particular had a profound effect on the early film industry, stretching the inventiveness of the companies to produce believable reportage, capture local colour and tell thrilling stories requiring complex staging. In this, the films took their cue – and much of their imagery – from pre-existing media. The illustrated press and magazines offered an array of material, from direct reporting and photography to sensational stories supported by sketches and paintings. As Richard Maltby notes:

> In popular journalism and fiction alike, imperial warfare was most frequently represented as an adventurous game of gallant charges, heroic retreats, lucky escapes, of pluck, grit and chivalry, in which guns flashed, cannons thundered and the bayonet made short work of the enemy.[34]

Some quite spectacular individual examples of films following this approach survive. Cavalry charges made for especially vivid films. At least two of these appear in the Lumière 1896 catalogue, and W. K. L. Dickson filmed several at a military review in Aldershot in July 1897. There are photographs of him with the huge Biograph camera, filming the various demonstrations from a platform (by special arrangement with his royal connections), and the very wide composition on the large-format film is beautifully clear throughout the long charge of the Cuirasseurs towards the camera. But Dickson's film is surpassed by Birt Acres' *Charge of the 12th Lancers* (1899). An advertisement by Acres' Northern Photographic Works trumpeted:

> To cinematographers. We have just secured the finest and most realistic military film ever taken... If you wish to electrify your audience, if you wish to double your takings, if you wish to prove yourself up to date, buy it ... Length 80ft. Price 40s.[35]

The surviving fragment justifies the hyperbole. Acres' camera position intensifies the speed of the oncoming charge, creating a sensation that the horses will burst out of the frame.

Marching, drilling, running up rigging, bringing field artillery to bear and a panoply of other displays all made for excellent films. Warships were another popular subject. Biograph's *Four Warships in Rough Seas* shows, in fact six, large battleships sailing in line, demonstrating the kind of ship 'ballet' associated with the numerous naval reviews intended to demonstrate Britain's maritime power. This particular occasion for the review may have been the Queen's Diamond Jubilee on 26th June 1897, or perhaps the final one of her reign in August 1899, presided over by the Prince of Wales. The scale of the ships, and the discipline of the line – filmed from the stern of one of the ships – is impressive, but the German Biograph company blew this out of the water with the most beautiful of early naval films, the *Battleship Odin Firing all Her Guns* (1900), apparently paid for by the Kaiser himself to show the world what German technology could do.[36] The great explosions of white smoke from the guns and the black smoke from the engines make for an aesthetically glorious image. All show, as it happened: the *Odin* never in her career fired a shot in anger.

Alfred West filming *Our Navy*, either in 1897 or 1907, when he is known to have shot further material.

All the major filmmakers were attentive to the enthusiasm for military spectacle. Whole series were dedicated to the Navy and Army. Alfred West's popular *Our Navy* (1898) was the first comprehensive compilation of minute-long military films. It covered the life of the navy from training recruits to the many specialist jobs that servicemen did. Several of these films survive, as well as a later illustrated catalogue of 1912 that describes the content of the show. As a Southsea photographer specialising in marine subjects, West was well placed to extend his interests to film – with permission from the naval authorities. He even received an invitation to present them to Queen Victoria at Osborne, with the Duke of York explaining them for her. The two-hour long standalone film show, supported with slides, songs and music, incorporated films of training, naval exercises and slices of life for the typical 'Jack Tar', including leisure time and dramatised scenes of courting and married life, which added some comic and sentimental interest.

Our Navy was shown regularly for several years in and around Portsmouth (then the Royal Navy's primary base), and had a summer residency at the Polytechnic lecture theatre in Regent Street, London for 14 years. At its height, the show had a staff of 50 and travelled to Canada, Australia and India.[37] There is evidence that the Admiralty and Navy League facilitated the Regent Street residency to encourage recruitment. Could such a show have survived financially so long without such support?

A review of a particular show at St James Hall, Piccadilly, is revealing about the reception of the films and their propaganda value:

> Scenes in the life of our sailors on board ship, e.g., seamen at drill, climbing the rigging on board the St Vincent, torpedo practice, etc., were vigorously applauded. The audience, however, were palpably bored at some still-life slides of the Duke of York's cabin, dining-room, etc., and audibly expressed their disapproval... What with Rudyard Kipling's vivid pen-pictures of the daily life on our warships and the exhibition of stirring cinematographs such as

R. W. Paul's 'Vaulting Horses' (1900) from his *Army Life* series.

were seen at St James's Hall, recruiting for the Navy ought to increase by leaps and bounds, and cause the Navy League to rejoice greatly.[38]

West followed up with *Our Army*, and his success was soon imitated by the big producers. Robert Paul's *Army Life* (1900) series of films served up a kind of meta-narrative of the ordinary soldier's life. Like West, Paul promoted it with a special illustrated booklet, and again we have some surviving film, including *Vaulting Horses*, a particularly well-composed exhibition of gymnastics at Aldershot, described in Paul's catalogue as 'one of the most striking and animated scenes it is possible to show... the whole of the film is filled with movement, the men working like clockwork.' At 80 shillings for 80ft, it was twice the price of most films of the time.[39]

Hepworth and the Warwick Trading Company produced series with similar subjects, such as drilling and exercises, which provided spectacle and inspired confidence in the physical fitness and training of the armed forces. As with West's over-arching narrative in *Our Navy*, the films often celebrated the service's past, with reminders of victories such as the Battle

Maxim, Firing Field Gun (Biograph, 1897).

of Trafalgar and of great commanders like Nelson, with occasional nods to the future. The Biograph Company's filmed demonstration of the Maxim machine gun by Hiram Maxim himself (*Maxim Firing Field Gun* (1897), is one of the most chilling of all the Victorian military films. Set up in a sunny field, the machine gun spits out lethal bullets at furious speed. It's impossible for today's viewer not to think of the slaughter of the First World War. At the time, however, it was a symbol of British technical innovation and superiority, as Hilaire Belloc's nasty little stanza had it: 'Whatever happens we have got / the Maxim gun, and they have not.'[40]

That sentiment, the breezy reliance on advanced weaponry or remembered triumphs, would come back to bite the British in the Boer War. The jingoism that the early film producers took such advantage of appears at this distance to be too feverish. The general population were more exposed and engaged with this war than previous conflicts due to newly available media such as popular papers like the *Daily Mail*, the illustrated press, war-related advertising campaigns and film. With the growth in public interest came the need to influence and direct it. The press baron Alfred Harmsworth noted that film had a particularly emotive effect on audiences. While readers usually forgot what they read in their daily newspapers, he wrote, 'no one can forget what he has seen on the screen.'[41] The propagandists did their work well, creating a suspenseful narrative of the war as a game to be won against a vilified enemy. The justification for the war however, failed to percolate down. One working-class woman called it 'a story book kind of a war. George and the Dragon stuff. We heard bits about individual bravery but we really had no idea why it was being fought.'[42]

The wild celebrations that greeted each small victory perhaps concealed an underlying public anxiety. But makers of moving images took advantage of the obsession – it was the integration of the nascent film business with the music hall that created the demand for war pictures of a certain type – and seized the opportunity for triumphalism, even to the point of incorporating symbolism into their films. Robert Paul's 'Grand Patriotic Trick Film', *Kruger's Dream of Empire* (1900), reflected the cartoonish images of heroes and villains found in the illustrated press and music hall sketches. It shows the South African leader Kruger gloating over his 1881 victory against the British, until a transformation occurs and he is shown the defeat of Majuba

Trafalgar Day in Liverpool (Mitchell and Kenyon, 1901).

Day in 1900. A statue of himself is magically replaced by a bust of Queen Victoria and British soldiers overcome him. From his corpse rises the image of Britannia in triumph.

The same national enthusiasm doesn't seem to have attached to the war that followed the Boxer rebellion in China – a more distant, more complex, more international affair. But films were made – mainly reconstructions – and surviving handbills and advertisements show that they were often screened alongside Boer War films. Joe Rosenthal, for Warwick, rushed off to China as soon as news of the uprising came through, but arrived after the main events – the killing of hundreds of western missionaries, the siege of the foreign legation in Peking (Beijing), the taking of Tientsin (Tianjin) and the lifting of the siege in August 1900. He took some films of military movements and some (illegal) footage of Russian-controlled Port Arthur, but concentrated his efforts on 'bread and butter' scenes of Chinese life for Warwick's catalogue. *Nankin Road Shanghai* survives of this series, showing among the local Chinese a troop of Sikh and German police, who were

Nankin Road, Shanghai (1900), filmed by Joe Rosenthal for Warwick Trading Co.

apparently necessary guards against potential crowd hostility at being photographed, which was common in the city at that time.

Contemporary photographs taken by Western journalists of the conflict stressed the brutality of the aftermath, most strikingly in the grisly reconstruction *Beheading of a Chinese Boxer* (1900). James Williamson's fictional *Attack on a China Mission* (1900) recreates the attempted massacre by Boxers of a missionary family. It is known nowadays for its novel use of shots and reverse shots. The central shot of the family being attacked by Boxers was filmed and released first; Williamson then added the arrival of the Bluejackets (naval soldiers) for the nick-of-time rescue. There seems to have been no reported case in which British troops rescued Christian missionaries – although the massacres were real enough – so Williamson's addition feels less like faithful reconstruction than wishful thinking. Perhaps it was tacit pressure from audiences, who found the idea of murder by 'cruel orientals' too alarming, that encouraged Williamson to supply an upbeat resolution. Filmmakers have wrestled ever since with the temptations of the happy ending.

Still photography had been used since the Crimean war to bring a sense of authenticity to reporting of Britain's imperial forces. Increasingly people expected to see as well as read about news, and a set of rules was beginning to develop about war reporting with respect to illustration that would in turn shape the way filmmakers chose to represent events. Anything controversial – images of the dead, the injured or those suffering from epidemic disease – was self-censored by filmmakers. Graphic images of this kind did appear in the illustrated magazines (such as *Black and White Budget*, which focused almost exclusively on the Boer War), but such images were considered inappropriate for the music hall or fairground show. Imagery of this kind, however true or informative was, if not directly 'censored', quite likely discouraged behind the scenes for reasons of national morale and taste.

Correspondents and photographers were what we would now call 'embedded' with the armed forces for practical reasons – safety, access to transport, supplies and information – and were consequently subject to controls. W. K. L. Dickson, with his small three-man team and hired Cape cart, was not an official correspondent in South Africa and wasn't eligible for army supplies, but he was still reliant on commanding officers for permissions to film any troop movements or actions. Generally he got what he asked for. He made good use of the voyage to the Cape with General Redvers Buller to secure general permission to travel, and attached himself to a naval unit right in the front line, hoping to secure pictures of the war in action. In his vivid account of his war experience, Dickson recalls facing the occasional irritation of the military command.[43] He must have frequently been in the way. The Biograph camera with its tripod was extremely bulky, heavy and difficult to manoeuvre. It required elevating and probably made considerable noise with its motors, making it a target for snipers. Being in the right place at the right time, with the right lighting conditions, was more or less impossible. The telescopic lens, on which Dickson relied for shots long enough and sharp enough to show real combat, was difficult to focus. It's difficult not to sympathise with his complaints about the clumsiness of 'the box', as they sometimes called it. But it was at least sturdy, as he recounts:

> Crash! Out we rush *en dishabille*, to find our two-wheeled vehicle fallen backward and our horses rearing and plunging around the debris. After politely

W. K. L. Dickson's *Rifle Hill Signal Corps* (1900).

reassuring the horses that the accident was due to the excessive weight of the Biograph and not their fault we brought the cart back into position and put the iron tripod on the shaft to keep it down. As usual the camera or Biograph remained uninjured. It seems to have a charmed life.[44]

Just as well: the team narrowly escaped being blown up on a river crossing as they accompanied Red Cross carts and endured such hazards as dysentery, hunger, floods, storms, tarantulas and scorpions, not to mention enemy fire.

The Naval brigade seem to have more or less adopted Dickson and his assistants, and the commanding officers could often be extremely amenable, allowing – whenever practical – the filming of troops and local men rebuilding blown-up bridges (*Repairing the Broken Bridge at Frere*, 1899), signal corps semaphoring from hill-top positions (*Rifle Hill Signal Corps*, 1899), naval guns firing in actual combat (*Guns Firing at Colenso*, 1899) and even the retreat from the *Battle of Spion Kop* (1900). This was hardly good

W. K. L. Dickson's *The Battle of Spion Kop* (1900).

propaganda for the Army, but it's one of the glories of Victorian film. Its breathtaking composition, which could only have been accomplished on the large-format camera, holds three distinct planes of action in perfect focus: the soldiers in the foreground trenches, the lines of horse drawn ambulances snaking into the distance and the outline of Spion Kop on the horizon.

If these films didn't quite show what many hoped to see, they were nonetheless lapped up by audiences in London and elsewhere, a mere three or four weeks after they were shot. The perils – let alone the costs – of covering the war express better than anything the ambition of the pioneer filmmakers for the new medium. Back at home, great value was placed on authenticity, which was measured by how close the filmmaker got to the action. Most highly prized was action that looked like it was taken during real combat, followed by films taken in real locations and with famous personalities. Genuine but background information on life in camp, exercises and manoeuvres was welcomed, and then there were recreations, which varied widely in their fidelity to actual events. In the illustrated magazines these ranged from photographs (real and staged) to sketches made by accredited correspondents during an action, to real stories embellished with drawings, to entirely fabricated tales of heroic deeds by British troops or of the enemy's dastardly deeds. The films reflected, in a simpler form, much the same set of representations. If a film had any claim on authenticity, the filmmaker would be sure to advertise this. The *Era*, for example, mentions a Biograph film of the popular Gordon Highlanders (a regiment that had distinguished itself only a month before in a heroic action at Dargai, near the Khyber Pass):

> Another exciting and interesting scene is a bayonet assault between some members of the camp at Aldershot. These scenes present soldier-life with a startling reality and fidelity which few can ever hope to see. They are not made up by persons disguised as soldiers, but taken from life, the principals being veterans in active service, who have "smelt powder" many times.[45]

Interest in the Imperial campaigns rose to new heights during 1899 and into 1900, but Dickson, Rosenthal and their peers had left South Africa after the relief of Ladysmith and the victory parades at Bloemfontein and Pretoria,[46] which made for an upbeat conclusion to an expensive and exhausting filmmaking tour. No filmmakers were present for the relief of Mafeking in May 1900, which caused near-hysterical rejoicing in the streets of Britain – much of it, perhaps, born of sheer relief at the successful defence of the Imperial enterprise in which people had invested so heavily (represented so well by the architecture, the pageantry, the industry we see in the films). It was only after the filmmakers had gone home that news of high casualties, concentration camps and the starvation of women and children began to filter through. The heroic, boys-own narrative sold to the British public for years began to ring hollow as it transpired that the Boers were braver, smarter and better equipped than their British counterparts. Enthusiasm for war

Mitchell and Kenyon's *Return of the Warwickshire Regiment* (1902).

films cooled, and by 1901 only the Biograph pictures at the Palace continued to draw regular audiences. The *Morning Post*, in its obituary for the Palace's manager Charles Morton in October 1904, attributed this against-the-tide success to his policy of even-handedness:

> He steered clear of all party questions and his house was not divided against itself... People who were not going out to the ordinary place of entertainment went to the Palace for information, well knowing that his politics and feelings would be respected.[47]

If the jingoism had abated by late 1901, military subjects could still make for popular films. The return of local regiments were events that filmmakers could profitably exploit, and the results illustrate how cameramen were learning to cover an event with multiple different shots and artistic compositions to enhance their coverage. Mitchell and Kenyon's *Return of the*

Warwickshire Regiment (made in 1902 but essentially similar to films of 1901) is a particularly fine example. The unedited films contain a variety of shots from positions along the processional route in Birmingham. A beautifully composed high-angle shot shows the imposing statues of Queen Victoria, flanked by Joseph Priestley and John Skirrow Wright, with a snaking path through which the troops would march through the cheering crowds. There are 'before' shots of the people getting into position and stewards and police arranging crowd barriers, a high-angle shot of the parade, and an experimental pan across the huge throng gathered for the event. An extraordinary shot of the serried ranks of soldiers, filling the frame in a grid formation, is a self-consciously crafted, even artistic treatment, and there is even an eye-level shot as if from the point of view of the spectators.

It's footage that wouldn't embarrass a news team today. The six rolls, totalling 14 minutes of film, were, in effect, a kit of parts for a type of longer, edited film that was still some years away, but they demonstrate a mode of thinking, an understanding of how people view films: the need for variety, for point of view, for movement, for pleasing or surprising angles – perhaps, even, for a type of film that makes the viewer aware of the filmmaker's presence. War reporting was a prime stimulus for the development of the newsreel but it influenced both propaganda and documentary too – Charles Urban, for example, covered the wars of the Victorian era and went on to work on the feature-length official documentary *The Battle of the Somme* (1916). Film historians have often been preoccupied with the development of narrative fiction film,[48] but the Victorian actuality film was at least as significant in setting the trajectory towards longer and more ambitious films, and in this the military subjects and series played a major part.

Close-up: The Pirates

There's a romance to the early days of any industry – full of invention, colourful characters and, usually, a fair amount of swashbuckling and sharp practice. The film industry was no exception. Competition between filmmakers was keen, and while remaking another manufacturer's films was routine, 'passing off' – what we'd now call piracy – was another matter. In the memoirs of Charles Urban is a lively account of his determination to stamp out illegal duplication of his films by his rival, Walter Gibbons:

> I succeeded in waylaying [A. D.] Thomas emerging from the Islington Empire after the show one night and hung on to him like 'grim death'... He was a big strong chap who could have made a nasty customer in a fight. We stopped the cab at Warwick Court, entered our office and while I put Thomas 'on his honour' I went into the packing room, got a chisel and a hatchet with some tacks which I showed to Thomas with the hint that I would not hesitate to use these tools, if he tried any nonsense. I told him we were bound for Chandos Street. He tried to assure me that Gibbons had given up the quarters, had removed all machines and developing equipment and that we would find an empty loft... The result of this search was three short duplicated films even bearing the Warwick trade mark at each beginning... Early next morning I took my evidence to the office of our company's solicitor and had a summons prepared.*

It seems like tough-guy Urban had Gibbons bang to rights, but such practice was no doubt common as demand for films outstripped supply. A recent discovery in the BFI National Archive's Victorian film collection appears to expose a similar act of industrial piracy. In the course of digitising the Archive's earliest films it became apparent that there were two copies of a film known as *A Morning Wash* (1900). One, a positive projection print, came from a collector of early film. The other was a roll of camera negative discovered in 1995 among the Mitchell and Kenyon collection. The film is attributed

---

* Charles Urban (ed. Luke McKernan), *A Yank in Britain: The Lost Memoirs of Charles Urban, Film Pioneer* (The Projection Box, 1999).

to Gibbons Bio-Tableaux, and there is good documentary evidence to support this. It features Gibbons himself and his chief operator, Jack Smith, as two men joshing about at their morning ablutions; Gibbons hands his mate boot blacking (polish) instead of the soap, with hilarious results.

Forensic examination of the two pieces of film revealed that the negative was the camera original and that the print could *only* have been made from this negative. It's unusual, if not unique, for both a print and its original negative from this era to survive, let alone from different sources. So what was the negative of a London filmmaker's work doing in Mitchell and Kenyon's Blackburn shop? Could it be that Gibbons was using M&K to print up both his own and other people's films, far from the prying eyes of the London trade? Was his friend A. D. Thomas the go-between as he travelled between north and south?

In any event, Gibbons, perhaps under threat of a writ, gave up the film game, married the daughter of a theatre magnate and inherited a huge music hall empire. The resilient Thomas, meanwhile, survived his tangle with authority and when, soon after, he went bankrupt, Urban gave him a job at the Warwick Trading Company. Piracy continued to dog the early film business, and filmmakers were forced to adopt ever more ingenious systems to combat it.

Walter Gibbons' *A Morning Wash* (1900); (right) negative version of the same film found in Mitchell and Kenyon collection.

THE SHOWMAN, July 5, 1901

Elocution Made Easy.

THE SHOWMAN

An Illustrated Journal for Showmen and all Entertainers.

VOL. II.—No. 31.   *All Rights Reserved.*   **JULY 5, 1901.**   [*Registered at the G.P.O. as a Newspaper.*]   TWOPENCE.

To Showmen.

The most popular Cinematograph Film in a Travelling Show is **ALWAYS A LOCAL PICTURE** containing Portraits which can be recognised. A Film showing workers leaving a Factory will gain far greater popularity in the town where it was taken than the most exciting picture ever produced. The workers come in hundreds, with all their friends and relations, and the Film more than pays for itself the first night. In other words this is

The Greatest Draw you can have,

. . AND IT IS . .

Our Business to Provide it

for you in Advance, for each Town you visit.

Write, for particulars and prices, to

HEPWORTH & CO.,

Telephone: No. 16, Walton-on-Thames.
Telegrams: "Hepworth," Walton-on-Thames.

Cinematographers, **Walton-on-Thames.**

London Agents—L. GAUMONT & Co., 25 Cecil Court, Charing Cross Road, W.C.

ENTERED AT STATIONERS' HALL.

Hepworth Local Film advert from *The Showman*, 5 July 1901.

5 THE GREATEST DRAW: LOCAL FILM

The rediscovery in the mid-1990s of the Mitchell and Kenyon films sent shockwaves through the community of silent film historians and enthusiasts.[49] This cache of some 900 rolls of uncut camera negatives dating from 1899 to 1913 had sat undisturbed in three metal milk churns in a Blackburn shop basement since the company ceased trading in the early 1910s. After a painstaking five-year restoration programme by the BFI National Archive, the films were unveiled: a variety of subjects – many of them miraculously well-preserved – made by partners James Mitchell and Sagar Kenyon, some for sale under their own Norden Films brand and others commissioned by showmen, for screening in fairground 'Bioscope' shows or by independent travelling exhibitors at town halls, theatres, institutes and assorted other venues.

Research into the collection, much of it involving marrying the films with contemporary reports and advertisements in local press, revealed a wealth of detail about the ways Mitchell and Kenyon and several other early filmmakers operated. Books, articles, cinema screenings and a four-part television series[50] won the films nationwide attention. Audiences responded with enthusiasm and wonder to something barely seen before: moving pictures of ordinary people in England's northern towns and cities at the dawn of the 20th century.[51] This was a significant rebalancing of the early film record away from the capital and the south. The spectacle of movement and faces from so long ago – what Tom Gunning calls 'the unending sea of humanity continually breaking against the camera'[52] – was no less fascinating for 21st century audiences than it was for those a century or more earlier.

Mitchell and Kenyon's moving images of Victorian Britain are now the most widely seen films of the era. For although the pair are routinely labelled 'Edwardian' filmmakers,[53] nearly a third of the Blackburn cache was made before our 1901 cut-off. Indeed, the sudden re-emergence of these films swells the ranks of surviving Victorian film by more than a quarter.

The discovery presented historians with a previously unknown film-making practice: what we now call local filmmaking. These were films taken in the locality of the show, with their primary audience the very people captured on the film. The cameramen would find a place and a time – the gates of a factory at lunchtime, a schoolyard at playtime or a church just after Sunday service – where they could get as many people as possible on camera, then hand out fliers inviting the same people to come and 'see how others see you'. During 1900 and 1901 this was a great craze – one perhaps invisible to the national press, but not to local newspapers, such as *The Hull Times*:

> Local pictures are all the rage this year. The cinematograph meets you at every turn, up-to-date and localised – you may even see the girls leaving Reckitt's starch factory.[54]

So why was local film so popular during this relatively short space of time? Local film was a sociable medium. It relied, like so many early film genres, on a simple observable effect. People in general are interested in themselves and evidently liked to see their own faces and their familiar environment on screen every bit as much as we do today. They liked to see people they knew, august members of society looking foolish, recognisable places. The overwhelming reaction documented in the few early press accounts was laughter: a common reaction, among children and adults alike, to the surprise of recognition. From the exhibitor's viewpoint, making an audience laugh was good for business. People would tell their friends what they had seen, increasing the audience at subsequent screenings. As an advertisement for Prestwich Company in *The Showman* put it:

> It is astonishing what a great attraction a local film is; crowds flock to see it, and there is generally some comical feature that causes much merriment.

Considerable delight is expressed as popular characters come on the screen, and great laughter as some grinning face appears.[55]

It was this ready audience that drew the filmmakers. They went to wherever local people congregated in significant numbers and filmed them; coming out of workplaces, at schools, at local sporting events, calendar customs, public celebrations of all kinds, at the seaside, or from the top of a tram in the high street. The films would be projected that night or the next, at the fair or a local hall, advertised as 'local films for local people'.

James Kenyon and Sagar Mitchell offered their own local filmmaking service (their advertising slogan was 'We take them and make them'), employing cameramen at 10s/6d per day and charging a fee per foot to the showmen for processing and printing. The filmmaking was often a team effort. In several of the films we can see Kenyon himself (though not Mitchell, as far as we can tell) directing the throng of workers exiting through the factory gates to stop them bunching up or standing still in front of the camera. In many cases – as in *20,000 Employees Entering Lord Armstrong's Elswick Works* or *Co-operative Wholesale*

Mitchell and Kenyon's *20,000 Employees Entering Lord Armstrong's Elswick Works* (1900).

Clothing Factory in Manchester (both 1900) – we can see the showman, too. Some showmen also performed this directorial function and had their own cameramen, using Mitchell and Kenyon only for processing and printing.

The earliest surviving British factory gate film is from early in 1900. The original inspiration was undoubtedly the Lumières' earliest film, *Sortie de l'usine* (*Workers Leaving the Lumière Factory*, 1895), but that was not exhibited as a local film in the way Mitchell and Kenyon's films were. While it was certainly shown to some of the brothers' factory workers in Lyon, it was then incorporated into their general programme for the élite audiences of Paris. Nevertheless, as we have seen, the Lumières quickly realised that local views fascinated audiences. Films taken locally by Lumière operators, such as *Entrée du cinematographe* at the Empire in Leicester Square and others in Vienna and elsewhere, were extremely popular and were soon widely imitated. One imitator was Robert Paul, who took several films on Brighton beach when he presented his Animatographe show at the Victoria Hall for the summer season of 1896. Local press remarked on their popularity with the local audience.

A few other examples of factory gate films survive, such as *Haggar's Bioscope Camera*, made around 1900, and the later *Works and Workers of Denton Holme* (1910). But the Mitchell and Kenyon cache proves just how prodigious a genre the local film was. The exhibition of local films was different to those early shows that formed part of a music hall variety bill. These were films of the working class for working-class audiences. Prices were low and audience numbers high. Fairground shows were short – 15 to 20 minutes, about the same duration as the music hall slot – but designed for the fast turnaround of the fairground attraction. The film show could be performed up to 20 times in a day. Haydon and Urry, Islington-based distributors of film and equipment, even offered film prints on thicker base for heavy use (this might partly explain why so few of the prints of local films survive: they were simply screened to death). Southern filmmakers like Cecil Hepworth and Paul tried to jump on this bandwagon, but the South lacked that connection between the factories and the fairs that made the Northern local film such a financial success.

No group of entrepreneurs was better suited to exploiting a craze than the fairground showmen. They were attuned to the shifting ground of public taste and could react with alacrity. Randall Williams was the first of the

Mitchell and Kenyon's *Sedgwick's Bioscope Showfront at Pendlebury Wakes* (1901).

showmen to invest in moving pictures: as early as the winter of 1896–97, when he trialled his show at the World's Fair in Islington (a trade show for travelling exhibitors) before opening at Norfolk's King's Lynn Fair later in 1897. Williams was one of very few touring showman at this time (perhaps the only one) who could command the considerable capital investment to mount one of these substantial shows. The fairground film shows could seat 500 to 1000 customers, and had spectacular show fronts featuring beautifully painted panels, live warm-up acts, barkers, interlocutors, musicians, projectionists with their equipment and numerous attendants, as well as illuminations, steam transport or horses. We can gauge the scale of a fairground film show from Mitchell and Kenyon's *Sedgwick's Bioscope Showfront at Pendlebury Wakes* (1901), while their later *Hull Fair* (1902) offers a glimpse of Randall Williams' own showfront, by then run by his descendants. And of course we know who the audience is, and how they appear, because we are looking at them. The filming process is also on display. The crowds are clearly directed in most cases, passing either side of the camera. The showmen are distinguishable from their dress and actions. Children stand directly at the front or cycle back after being shooed away. They jostle to be close to the camera. Their personalities come through; the shy and the curious, the blank and the brash, defiantly posed.

'Town Hall' shows were larger, longer and more ambitious productions. A good example is the show mounted at a large multipurpose theatre in Bradford by independent exhibitor A. D. Thomas. *Crowds outside St George's Hall in Bradford* (1901) shows a dense mass of people, many of them boys, on a wet February afternoon waiting to see a matinee performance of films of the wars in South Africa and China, as well as local subjects. According to the press reports the show was a full entertainment lasting two hours, incorporating songs, music supplied by local regimental bands and commentary. The live acts, however, were there to support the films, just as they were for

Mitchell and Kenyon's *Crowd Entering St George's Hall, Bradford* (1901), with A. D. Thomas in homburg hat near top right corner.

'An Utter scamp': A. D. Thomas filming *Torpedo Flotilla Visit to Manchester* (1901).

Alfred West's *Our Navy* show of 1898: the film show now had enough pull to get big audiences over and over again, even outside of a conventional variety programme. Thomas's film, taken in the afternoon of people waiting to get in to the 3pm show, was shown at the evening performance and in subsequent days to persuade people to come back and see the show again. We get a brief glimpse of Thomas himself, instructing the men who are whipping up the crowd during the filming. His character is evident in those few seconds: decisive, flamboyant, skilled at putting people at ease and making them laugh.

Thomas was perhaps closer to a boxing promoter than to a film entrepreneur like Charles Urban. He seems to have been as engaging a self-promoter as you could hope for from a Victorian showman. Cecil Hepworth remembered him as:

> an utter scamp, a very loveable fellow and one of the greatest showmen who ever lived. He was actively, extremely actively, engaged in the cinematograph

business. He plastered the whole town wherever he went, and he went nearly everywhere, with tremendous posters in brilliant colours describing his wonderful shows and his still more wonderful self... Less honestly... he would parade the town in person, mounted high on an open lorry actively turning his camera on every little knot of people he passed. As the lorry was plastered with his colourful posters telling them to come and see themselves at such-and-such a hall tonight... Unfortunately for their hopes the camera had no film in it.[56]

But we should not confuse the travelling showman with his hyperbole; these were, for the most part, astute, hard-working businessmen. Thomas was extremely energetic, covering a considerable territory and undertaking personal financial risk. He was inventive with publicity, constantly refreshing advertising and finding little tricks to pull in audiences. The punters weren't paying much (between 3d and 1s), so, unlike the big city centre music halls, Thomas had to work hard for big audiences every time. At his peak he was running shows simultaneously in several different towns and cities. The investment in staff and equipment was considerable but the profits seem to have been good; the Newcastle shows, run by his brother Issac, brought in £100 a week on their own. He delegated certain shows and functions to competent men, who would build their own film careers, but he was constantly active himself. We can see him directing operations in several films, among them *Manchester Street Scenes*, *Torpedo Flottila visit to Manchester*, and *Manchester and Salford Harriers' Cyclists Procession* (all 1901). He commissioned or was involved in at least 130 titles in the Mitchell and Kenyon collection and with dozens more commissioned from Hepworth, and probably others besides, it's clear he was a significant producer in the Victorian era.

Thomas's success, however, proved temporary. Heavily invested in multiple touring shows, he found himself exposed when public tastes changed. The local films had been something he could control (unlike the supply of topicals from the main film companies), but they were no longer enough of a draw by 1902 to sustain his particular kind of show. While competing shows, such as Alfred West's *Our Navy* or Paul's *Army Life*, could be screened repeatedly over months or years, Thomas's were tied to a moment – public obsession with the Boer War in particular. Before the end of 1902 he would file for bankruptcy with £9,000 worth of debt.[57] He sold his business to his friend Walter Gibbons and continued to work in the film business for a while with Charles Urban, despite their earlier differences (see 'Close-up', pp. 80–1). For a time Thomas made films in Canada, where he had family, then he re-emerged intermittently, in Durham in 1903 and again in Manchester in 1905 under a new banner, the Royal Canadian Animated Picture Co., claiming that his pictures of the Royal visit to Manchester and Salford were under royal patronage, which seems characteristically brazen.

Like the facial comedy or the panorama, the local film seems very much part of the novelty phase of film. They were made to be simple attractions. Once the novelty wore off, filmmakers stopped making them in significant numbers. But despite their brief existence we can observe some advances in technique and organisation. The techniques honed here would become the bedrock of newsreel production from the 1910s onwards, and television historians might see in these films the roots of outside broadcast filming. In location work of this type, Victorian filmmakers had to work with existing settings and lighting conditions, and were forced to develop strategies to deal with all eventualities. They learned flexibility and discovered what worked in terms of this apparently simple form, carefully selecting the best camera positions to capture the crowds and show them to dramatic effect, as in *Great Northern Railway Works at Doncaster* (1900), in which the exiting workers flow directly at us over a bridge. And they filmed impressive establishing shots such as the one in *Workers at Kynoch Ltd. Lion Works, Birmingham* (1901), in which the name of the factory and the carved Lion are emblazoned against the sky.

But there are other features of these local films that might change how we think of them in relation to 21st century film forms. We can see in them the kind of informal amateur film that we might take ourselves on a mobile phone or share on TikTok or YouTube, and they seem very far from what we think of as 'documentary' film. Certainly the function of the local film was 'to present, rather than to represent, to show, rather than to narrate',[58] but there was a degree of directorial intervention in the films. The filmmakers wrangled the crowd rather than just passively filming them; creating movement, making people laugh and wave, and placing individuals or small groups as motionless focal points to enhance the three-dimensional quality of the film (girls in white dresses worked well). Occasionally a showman tried to instigate a fight where

North Sea Fisheries, North Shields (1901).

the location suggested a belligerent crowd, such as the famously pugnacious trawlermen in *North Sea Fisheries, North Shields* (1901). It may not be quite the 'creative treatment of actuality' John Grierson had in mind in his famous definition of documentary film but perhaps this is just a question of degree.

For modern audiences, the local film has effectively become 'documentary' in its simplest historical sense. The workplace films are particularly fascinating, giving us, 120 years or more later, a rare view of people in their everyday garb and working environment. For Paul Dave, 'rather than confirming what we thought we knew about northernness and class, the early cinema genre of the factory gate administers a shock to such assumptions.'[59] Comparing their representations of English 'northernness' with the paintings of L. S. Lowry, Dave sees aesthetic choices in many of these rapidly-made films. Dave sees the films as a means of rediscovering how the workforce of the industrial north saw itself at the end of the Victorian era: forward-looking, progressive, utopian and 'open to the future', not at all the failed and defeated 'lonely crowd' that some contemporary critics have attributed to Lowry's representations. The factory gate and other local films offer us a unique opportunity to study the behaviour of the crowd – England's industrial north is often characterised by its crowds [60] – and those who filmed them. Something about the unstudied movement of the people *en masse* is particularly affecting: they seem so natural and alive.

The factory workers captured in these films were generally not people who had time to write their reminiscences, and no journalists asked them what they thought as they might today. So we have no first-hand reports, but recognising oneself on screen must have been a striking and memorable experience at a time when most people had few photographs and even mirrors were comparatively rare. The first 'movie stars' were still more than a decade away, and there was no expectation that a film would survive beyond its own particular moment in time. The attraction of the local film for its participants, then, has nothing to do with the desire for universal recognition or fame – the Hollywood fantasy of two decades later. Even so, for a couple of short years the people were the stars of the show.

Close-up: The Kid Stays in the Picture

Making eye contact with someone from 120 years or more ago is a distinctly odd experience. When a young boy – 8 or 9 years old – stares into a lens and into your eyes across space and time, it can feel for a moment like a real connection. But this is fleeting; as soon as that fugitive sensation passes, you can study his face directly, in that voyeuristic way we have with film, and curiosity sets in.

I have my favourites, most of all the Mitchell and Kenyon film *Workforce Leaving Alfred Butterworth and Sons, Glebe Mills* (1901). I'm not alone: it gives the clearest view of kids hanging around in front of the camera as

the Lancashire mill disgorges its workers at midday. The children come up to the camera – some bashful, some bold. Girls glance sideways at the camera then look away. One lad strikes a confident, even belligerent pose, thumbs in waistcoat pockets. Another just stands and watches, a picture of innocent, boyish curiosity. That's my boy.

We can speculate what he's looking at. A cameraman turning the crank on his Model 4 Prestwich camera, perhaps some assistants, and the showman who is making this film to show at Oldham fair. Maybe he sees James Kenyon or Sagar Mitchell in the flesh. There's a hint of a smile now and then on his otherwise expressionless face, so perhaps A. D. Thomas is pulling silly faces, as he would likely do to get a reaction for the camera. Other than that, the boy can see the receding backs of mill hands rushing away down a cobbled street with a long brick wall. They are off to get their lunch, or preoccupied with thoughts of the 'going-off money' for the coming holidays. Maybe it's Wednesday, pay day at Glebe Mills.

Why does he stay there so long? The smarter kids will have worked it out – they know their faces will be in the animated photographs showing at the Wakes fair, so they are making sure they'll be seen. They just want to be recognised, but chance has made them immortal.

It's impossible not to speculate. What is his life like? Is he working – a half-timer perhaps? What are his prospects? What kind of house does he live in? The area around Glebe Mills, with chimneys poking up like islands in an ocean of brick? What does his future hold? Will he work at the Mills? Little chance of him dodging the draft in 1916, when he will be in his early twenties; is *his* one of the 72 names on the Glebe Mills Roll of Honour? A new housing estate now stands in place of the mill: only the name 'Glebe Street' and this film survive.

OPPOSITE: Mitchell and Kenyon's *Workforce Leaving Alfred Butterworth* (1901).

6 MOVING IMAGES: PANORAMAS, PHANTOM RIDES AND TRAVEL

Moving pictures were *made* for vicarious travel. Captivating views, scenes of foreign lands and local sights, and journeys on boats, trams or trains were very prominent in early film catalogues. Travel films provided picturesque views and, when coupled with camera movement created a pleasurable sensation of momentum, like a gentle version of a fairground ride. It might seem an obvious idea to mount the camera on a moving object in order to exploit film's inherent qualities (if you could keep it stable enough), but we have Frenchman Alexander Promio to thank for the first one, *Panorama du Grand Canal pris d'un bateau,* taken on 25 October 1896 from a gondola in Venice, Europe's most desirable tourist site.

It was Promio's bosses, the Lumière brothers, who labelled it a 'panorama', evoking the entertainments so beloved of 19th century audiences. These were spectacular 'realistic' paintings of cityscapes exhibited in a huge rotunda such as Barker's Panorama in Leicester Square – so vertiginous in scale that the visiting Queen Charlotte was overcome with queasiness (still a common complaint for IMAX and Virtual Reality viewers). Wyld's Great Globe, another tourist attraction which sat in Leicester Square from 1851 to 1862, was a geographic 'experience' representing in its multi-floored convex space the entire surface of the world, in relief'. Interest in travel and geography was booming.

The early 19th century saw the development of 'moving panoramas', in which a set of views painted on a rolled-up cloth (an exotic landscape, a great battle) were unfurled before the audience as a commentator explained the

Panoramic View of Conway on the L. & N.W Railway (Biograph, 1898).

scene. These popular shows toured widely and, as John Plunkett has suggested, fostered in the public a 'picture-going' habit long before the arrival of film.[61]

Other filmmakers soon followed Promio's lead, assured of a ready audience. Over the next few years an astonishing number of panoramas were filmed, all over the world. The panorama enabled filmmakers to exploit existing interest in subjects such as the great cities – where the film shows were first exhibited – improving on the filmed movement of people in front of buildings and monuments by the movement of the camera through the space. In less busy surroundings, the recreation of the sensory experience of gentle travel by boat or barge or tram was both mesmerising and enjoyably immersive. Panoramas were sensitively composed pictures of beautiful places, with careful attention to depth, clarity, detail and lighting effects. In narrative terms they were interesting and lively. A film panorama offered many of the benefits of travel without the discomfort, the investment of time or the cost. Filmmakers extended their range of subjects along the lines of pre-existing popular subjects in the painted panoramas, photographs, magic lantern slides and stereographs. They followed the well-trodden routes of trade, commerce and tourism, filming views of Venice, Paris, New York or London, and less accessible sites such as the temples of ancient Egypt, the Swiss Alps or the Ghats of Varanasi. They took much the same pictures, from much the same standpoints, as the illustrators and guidebooks had before them. The sheer number of these films produced over many years testifies to their popularity with audiences.

In 1897 a new and sensational variant of the panorama emerged. It was the Lumière brothers, once again, who are believed to be have been first to release a film taken from a moving train. The first-ever such 'phantom ride' (although it wasn't given that label) went backwards: *Départ de Jerusalem en chemin de fer* (*Leaving Jerusalem by Railway*, 1897) was taken from the rear platform of the train as it pulled out of the station. It's a very effective film. The people nearest to the train look straight at the camera, smiling then waving as the train draws away. As it gathers speed, the passengers further up the platform don't notice the camera, so the viewer sees them in a more detached way, as part of a complex scene of people, buildings and landscape.

The phantom ride, as a form, neatly illustrates the immersiveness of moving pictures. Victorian audiences would have *felt* its effects.[62] The earliest known use of the phrase in Britain is around 1897, when the American Mutoscope and Biograph Company's *Haverstraw Tunnel* is described as '*The* phantom ride'. The phrase soon became generic. This film view is forward-facing, taken from the front of the train and giving a driver's perspective of the tracks and the dramatic plunge into the darkness of a tunnel. The *Evening Standard* enthused: 'a more exciting and sensational piece of realism has never been presented to an audience.'[63]

The British Mutoscope and Biograph Company, founded in London in mid-1897 partly on the back of successes like *Haverstraw Tunnel*, began to make more phantom rides by arrangement with British railway companies such as the London and North Western. Its series featuring the 'Irish Mail', a

The Irish Mail Taking up Water at Full Speed (British Biograph, 1898).

glamorous express train which ran from the capital to the port of Holyhead, vary from the sedately paced *Panoramic View of Conway Castle on the L. & N.W. Railway* (1898) to the breakneck *The Irish Mail Taking up Water at Full Speed* (1898), filmed from a train running alongside the express. Taken on large 68mm format, they are among the most beautiful and thrilling films from this era. Biograph's W. K. L. Dickson was something of a specialist in train films – one of his most spectacular was the *Empire State Express* (US, 1896), showing this huge train pounding towards the audience at an oblique angle, which though less than a minute long, took five days to achieve. These films were not simple to shoot; they were just as carefully considered as such filming is today, and required painstaking set up and negotiation. For the Irish Mail films, the railway company made an extra carriage available for the camera and crew in exchange for informal publicity.

The phantom ride was a highly adaptable genre, exploiting not only the natural drama of the trains themselves, but all of the views of places and people that train travel could reveal. Alexander Promio, who was in London in June 1897 for the Jubilee, returned in October, when he took a series of films of the Thames for Lumière, including *Panorama de Westminster pris de la Tamise*, shot from a boat. He then travelled to Dublin via Liverpool, where he took a series of four films from the then-new elevated railway, later nicknamed the 'Docker's Umbrella' (see also Mitchell and Kenyon's *Employees Leaving Alexandra Docks, Liverpool*, 1901), travelling through the extraordinary landscape of the great Merseyside docks. This must have been filmed in sections, as the amount of stock in the cinematograph camera was limited.

Others quickly jumped on the bandwagon. On 16 April 1897 the *Era* carried an advertisement for Chard's Vitagraph announcing *Through Chiselhurst Tunnel on the S.E.R.* as 'the only English phantom ride', but by 1898 it was a crowded field. Robert Paul's sadly lost but thrilling sounding film, *On a Runaway Motor Car through Piccadilly Circus* (1897), may have been the first phantom ride to use 'undercranking' to speed up the action – a device much copied by later filmmakers. Cecil Hepworth took several picturesque phantom rides in the South West of England in 1898: *View from an Engine Front* from Barnstaple to Ilfracombe and the famous *View from an Engine Front – Shilla Mill Tunnel* and *View from an Engine Front – Train Leaving Tunnel*, later used to bookend G. A. Smith's *The Kiss in the Tunnel* (1899). For sheer Victorian eccentricity, it would be hard to beat the Brighton and Rottingdean Seashore Electric Railway, a sea-going train carriage on stilts known as 'Daddy Long Legs', filmed in 1897 for Paul's Theatrograph. Mitchell and Kenyon took several long sequences, including *A Cinematographic View of the Royal Albert Bridge* (1901), a combination of panorama and phantom ride that takes in the whole of Plymouth Harbour and shows a variety of shipping vessels, from a mid-19th century wooden hulk used for training cadets to the latest battleships and packet steamers. Perhaps the most stunning is Biograph's *Panoramic View of the Vegetable Market at Venice* (1898), filmed with the large-format 68mm camera on a curving trajectory from a motorised yacht on the Grand Canal, giving a slight stereoscopic effect.

The panoramas and phantom rides of Victorian film very much reflected world-changing advances in transportation: the extension of the railway

Panoramic View of the Vegetable Market at Venice (Biograph, 1898).

network, the development of the London Underground, the expansion of coastal and international shipping routes, the electrification of the trams in 1901/02, and the coming of the motor car. And it was via these networks that the earliest British film companies, sent cameramen out into the world to capture views of places that audiences might otherwise never see. Robert Paul and Birt Acres were first in the field. Acres had taken a film of Niagara Falls in 1895 (which survives as a very short view), while Paul sent cameraman Henry Short on a tour of Portugal and Spain in 1896. From this series we have *A Sea Cave Near Lisbon,* held as an exemplar of the 'new travel film' by Rachael Low and Roger Manvell:

> It is a small step from the view of Whitehall to the view of Paris, the Norwegian fjord or Niagara Falls from the point of view of the camera, but from the point of view of the audience the service of the motion picture to the widening of experience was immense.[64]

Panorama of the Druidical Monuments at Stonehenge (Warwick Trading Co., 1901).

This 'widening of experience', and the observably greater feeling of realism offered by moving pictures, as opposed to still images, was stressed in the filmmakers' catalogues. Even where the film tackled a static subject, such as city architecture or a monument, they would accentuate other effects that gave their film an edge over a photograph. In *Panorama of the Druidical Monuments at Stonehenge* (1900), the camera can simply encompass more of the view of the stones. Though more immersive, it imitates the photographs or stereographs of the time by including, essentially for scale, two figures, a policeman and a woman.

Panoramas were described in the catalogues according to the particular effect that film gave – as here, for Hepworth's *Thames River Scenery* (1900):

> The latter portion of the picture shows a long panorama of a great number of beautifully decorated house-boats of all designs and sizes... the effect of the sunlight on the rippling water is very beautifully rendered, and the scene is one of much interest and animation.'[65]

Others, like *Panoramic View of the Vegetable Market at Venice*, could show the slight stereoscopic effects conveyed by the camera movement. Hepworth described this effect in a series of scenes collectively titled *Panorama of the Paris Exhibition* (1900), capturing images of the *Exposition Universelle de Paris* from a boat on the Seine:

> Buildings of all descriptions are seen; from the Eiffel Tower and the wonderful erection forming the Schneider exhibit, to the merest palace of amusement, and marvellous, stereoscopic relief is yielded by the buildings, at different distances, passing one another at varying rates.'[66]

Describing another view, he stresses how the depth of field, in movement, adds to the mystery, giving enticing glimpses of wonders beyond: 'At all times the intervals between the buildings afford glimpses of the most distant portions of the vast exhibition'.[67]

Hepworth's *Panorama of the Paris Exhibition, No. 3* (1900).

The Paris *Exposition* that ushered in the 20th century was a remarkable event for many reasons, not least a multitude of different applications for novelty moving pictures, including phantom rides and panoramas: from the Lumières' projection onto the world's largest screen (21 x 16m) to Raoul Grimoin Sanson's simulated ride using film shot from an ascending and descending hot-air balloon. Less elaborate, but no less effective, were the many films taken of the buildings and people, most of which were panoramas or variations of the phantom ride. James White, for Edison, took a kind of vertical phantom ride film in the ascending elevator of the Eiffel Tower, giving a bird's eye of the exhibition site, as well as film of the famous moving walkway, bringing the visitors past the camera. A cameraman for Warwick took a 360-degree pan of the Exposition's wedding-cake pavilions from the Champ de Mars (*Panorama around the Eiffel Tower* [1900]). As with Queen Victoria's Diamond Jubilee, all the world's major film companies covered this momentous event, and many of their films survive.

Panoramas and phantom rides became a staple device for the travel films that flourished in the Victorian era. Initially a novelty, then a fad, the panorama and the phantom ride ultimately became incorporated into film grammar as, respectively, the panning shot and the travelling shot. To differentiate itself from the magic lantern and painted panoramas, the film needed to move on from that 'best seat in the house' forward-facing position, which it did to an extent by moving the camera, and thereby the spectator's perspective, through space.

However, travel films did adopt the model of the magic lantern show by producing series or 'tours' of foreign lands. G. A. Smith and Charles Urban travelled together to film an entire tour of Italy. The one surviving print, *A Visit to Pompeii* (1901), is eight minutes long and consists of two of the films spliced together in the sequence in which they appear in the Warwick catalogue. The first, a full 360-degree pan made possible by new revolving heads for the camera tripod, showed the ancient ruins – then still being excavated – with workmen and tourists giving scale to the images. In the distance we can see Vesuvius smoking through the heat haze. This is the destination for the following film, in which we ascend the great volcano itself. In one of the finest shots in Victorian film, we see the ground fall away as the camera films from the rear of the funicular railway.

Visit to Pompeii (Warwick Trading Co., 1901).

Much of the globe would be covered, and whenever world events focused attention on a particular area cameramen would use the opportunity to film local landmarks and customs. The catalogues of Warwick, Robert Paul and Hepworth are full of multi-film series taken by intrepid cameramen, some of whom became quite famous. The myth of the heroic cameraman starts here: operators recklessly strapped themselves to the front of speeding trains and filmed under treacherous conditions in remote regions. Perhaps the most spectacular extant film is from Joe Rosenthal's China series for Warwick Trading Company. *Ride on the Peak Tramway* (1900) takes us on a 400-metre drop down the vertiginous Hong Kong funicular. The sole surviving print is in poor condition, but as the tram crests the peak it's just possible to see the huge vista of Victoria Harbour and Kowloon laid out before us, as if viewed from the world's greatest natural rollercoaster.

Closer to home, audiences delighted in seeing their own neighbourhood on screen in a phantom tram ride, as Mitchell and Kenyon, among others,

Trip to Vesuvius (Warwick Trading Co., 1901).

well understood. Some of these phantom rides had a topical hook, such as the opening of a newly electrified tram route. Surviving films such as Mitchell and Kenyon's *Ride on a Tram through Belfast* (1901) or Biograph's stunning *Panorama of Ealing from a Moving Tram* (1901) capture the idle pleasures of watching the world go by, but viewed today, the preserved details of their moving scenes, with their shop fronts and people busy about their days, allow us to experience something close to time travel.

The concept of time travel had been popularised by HG Wells' 'The Time Machine', published in 1895 and conceived before projected film was a reality. Later the same year, R. W. Paul, in partnership with Wells himself, attempted to patent an idea for a kind of 'ride', apparently using techniques similar to those later associated with the panorama and phantom ride. It was imagined as a carriage accommodating multiple viewers, simulating Wells' machine with realistic movement – acceleration, deceleration, sideways and up and down motion. A panoply of effects – sound, wind and visual imagery – added to the atmosphere. Ahead of the passengers would be a screen showing scenes of other eras, as if they were travelling forward or backwards in time. The creators even incorporated a favourite showman's trick of appearing to lose control, as the conductor would 'overshoot' on the return trip to the present, pretending to be lost in the age of the dinosaurs. Sadly, the idea – a prototype Virtual Reality machine – proved far ahead of its time.

Writing in 1948, Low and Manvell said of the travel film:

> these films are the ones which are most full of interest to us seeing them some fifty years later. They form the first chapter in the recording of history in the motion picture and for this reason alone these prints that have survived will be treasured and preserved and reprinted for future generations of students.[68]

Over 70 years on, the value of these films has only increased, not just as records of the first motion pictures but as records of a lost era. Victorian filmmakers tried every trick they knew to fully explore three-dimensional space, infusing their films with movement and interest. Today these films, like Paul's unrealised vision, offer another dimension: transporting us back in time.

Montage: The Phantom Ride

By mounting the camera on a tram, boat or train, phantom rides gave Victorian viewers a thrilling sense of momentum, whatever their velocity.

First appearing in Britain in 1898, they rapidly became a favourite cinematic genre.

Top to bottom: *View from an Engine Front – Shilla Mill Tunnel* (1899); *Irish Mail Taking up Water* (1898); *Beautiful Panorama of Railway from St. Germans Mill Bay* (1900); *Trip to Vesuvius* (1901); *View from an Engine Front – Barnstaple* (1898).

Top to bottom: *Tram Ride through Southampton* (1900); *Panorama of Ealing from a Moving Tram* (1900); *A Ride on the Peak Tramway* (1900); *Thames River Scenery – Panorama of the Crowded River* (1899); *Four Warships in Rough Seas* (1900).

Close-up: Researching Victorian film

Identifying Victorian films can involve dogged detective work. Often, the films survive only as fragments, and have no identifying titles. By the time they are acquired by an archive, provenance may have been lost and information may be sketchy. Once the work of examining the film for forensic clues has (hopefully) narrowed down the possibilities, filmographic research can begin. The best sources – when they survive – are the filmmakers' or distributors' catalogues, where we can try to match the film's content with a synopsis.

Digitised newspapers, now relatively accessible, may contain notices about films advertised for sale or as part of a music hall programme. Photo-

Queen Victoria's Diamond Jubilee – Queen in Carriage (1897).

Unidentified film known as *Footpads* (c. 1896).

graphic journals such as *The British Journal of Photography* and magazines such as the *Harmsworth Magazine* carry useful information about early film shows, while films are frequently mentioned in contemporary press such as *The Era*, the main trade paper for the music hall and entertainment world. Local shows might be listed in *The Showman*, a paper for touring fairground exhibitors. Marketing materials such as handbills or personal memoirs left by filmmakers are particularly rare, though a few survive.

Sometimes we have to make a guess based on a film's subject or location. One of the many views of Queen Victoria's Diamond Jubilee was identified recently with the aid of online street views, the souvenir programme of the parade to identify troops and positioning of military bands along the route, and the catalogue of Alfred Wrench, which advertised his film of the Queen's coach in King William Street.

A film about a street robbery, acquired by the BFI National Archive with no accompanying provenance, is catalogued as *Footpads*, and tentatively dated 1897. The original print's square frame edges and small perforations suggest that it may have been made by Robert Paul, and it was acquired with two known Paul films. But nothing like it appears in any Paul catalogue, and nothing in the contemporary press gives us a lead. It's the kind of mystery the early film researcher must get used to.

7 NEW PERSPECTIVES: ART AND SCIENCE

In May 1899, in one of her last public engagements, Queen Victoria visited the site of one of her most treasured legacies. The day marked the commencement of work on a new set of buildings for the South Kensington Museum – now renamed Victoria & Albert Museum – the great collection of scientific, industrial and decorative arts (including photography, for which Prince Albert and the Queen were particular enthusiasts), which its founders wished to be a source of inspiration to craftsmen and industry. This was part of the museum complex affectionately known as 'Albertopolis', funded by the proceeds of the Great Exhibition of 1851 organised by the Prince. The museums were to have days with free entry and late-night opening so that working people could come and study their collections. This was the manifestation of his aspirations for a German style of education, and it encapsulated the grand Victorian project to discover, collect and catalogue everything from the glories of the natural world, to human artistic and technological achievements, to the spoils of imperial conquest, and then to display it for the improvement of the nation.

There were filmmakers present that day, primarily to record the presence of the Queen. The Biograph Company's *Her Majesty the Queen Arriving at South Kensington on the Occasion of the Laying of the Foundation Stone of The Victorian and Albert Museum, 17th May 1899* shows Victoria in her carriage, but it doesn't stay for her speech, in which she expressed her great hopes for this bequest to her subjects:

> My interest in this great Institution, which, in its inception and during its early days, I shared with My dear Husband, has grown with its progress and development; and I rejoice that I have been able to take a personal part in the completion of a Scheme which will be not the least Distinction of My Reign, and which will, I trust, continue to be a powerful factor in the industrial enlightenment and the artistic training of My people.[69]

The hard divide between 'industrial enlightenment' and 'artistic training' – between science and the arts – was only beginning to form at the end of the Victorian era. The new 'V&A' buildings marked a new stage in the increasing separation of the museum's art and science collections; it would be another decade before the Science Museum as a wholly distinct entity was constituted.

Early filmmakers were no more preoccupied with such distinctions than anybody else. Film slotted quite naturally in to the more educational side of the entertainment business, and both art and science were ideal themes. The 1890s lecture scene was lively, appearing in the large music halls as well as among the programmes of talks and exhibitions held in the mechanics institutes, literary and philosophical societies, town halls and clubs up and down the land. Exhibitors used the words 'scientific' and 'artistic' as promotional terms in a society that prided itself on self-improvement and education. Lectures had for decades used various types of projected illustrations, from lantern slides to moving panoramas, and film became another tool in the lecturer's kit.

Initially, the film show appeared in this schedule of public events as a demonstration of technological advance in itself. But as with the highly decorated machines of the Victorian era, the exhibitors simultaneously had an eye to aesthetics. The natural world in particular seemed an arena in which art and science could meet, and the power of film as an observational tool was keenly felt by audiences from the very first projected shows.

The recording of natural movement is, of course, intrinsic to film. But for audiences seeing film for the first time, the movement itself was the attraction, and one class of films stands out in the Victorian era and is all-but unique to it: the 'sea waves' film. A contemporary newspaper report of a film show at the Liverpool Amateur Photographic Association captures something of the effect of such films on their audience:

Cecil Hepworth's *Rough Seas Breaking on Rocks* (1899).

> It is not too much to say that persons seated near the screen must have shrunk from the approaching billows which gathered, lifted their foam-tossed crests, curled and crashed down with an absolute realism from which nothing was wanted but the roar.[70]

Nearly every report of early film screenings mentions audience reaction to films of sea waves. Films showing the movement of water were very popular for their mesmeric effect as well as for the initial shock they gave audiences at their feeling of 'absolute realness'. The film that so impressed the Liverpool audience was Birt Acres' *Rough Sea at Dover*, made in spring of 1895, during his short partnership with Robert Paul, for the copies of Kinetoscope machines that Paul was then manufacturing. It shows large waves breaking in satisfyingly dramatic fashion on the Kent port's Admiralty Pier. The surviving print is quite blurry (there are contemporary accounts that films made for the Kinetoscope were comparatively dim) but it was clearly impressive in its day. We are lucky to have an account of Acres showing the film when he demonstrated his Kineopticon projector at the prestigious Royal Photographic Society on 14th January 1896. His demonstration was part of the light relief entertainment rather than a formal paper, but it was reported with great enthusiasm by *Amateur Photographer*'s reporter:

> the final slide – a study of waves breaking on a stone pier – was simply wonderful in its realistic effect. We all know how beautiful ordinary instantaneous effects of breaking waves appear on the screen but when the actual movement of nature is reproduced in addition the effect is little short of marvellous. Very rarely indeed has such enthusiastic applause as greeted Mr Acres upon the conclusion of his demonstration been heard at the 'Royal'.[71]

Photographic film, whether still or moving, loves water. Victorian photographers had incorporated every aspect of its reflective qualities into their picturesque aesthetic – particularly prizing the capturing of the perfect moment. Moving pictures went one better; the unpredictable movements of sea waves or waterfalls showed off the new medium better than any other subject. The audience were already familiar with natural views from countless paintings, lantern slides, stereoscopic views and postcards, but the hypnotic quality of movement was clearly compelling. The sensation of movement that the moving image can create is as pleasurable to us today as it was to our Victorian forbears. The feeling is more akin to the contemplation of art, staring at waves lapping on a beach or watching the countryside roll by from the window of a train. But although early sea wave films may share a kinship with later art film, it's probably unwise to assume any intent on behalf of the early filmmaker to produce an artwork, rather than an aesthetically pleasing entertainment.

Of all the pioneers, perhaps only Birt Acres had such direct artistic aspirations. As a semi-professional photographer, he had entered competitions for shots that best captured the movement of water: a feat that had been eluding painters for centuries. Producers of magic lantern slides made their own attempts, with scenes of ships at sea in which lighting effects could be

A Sea Cave Near Lisbon (Henry Short for Paul's Animatograph Works, 1896).

changed in a 'slipping slide' transition from a sunny day and flat calm, to a raging torrent threatening imminent shipwreck.

By the 1890s instantaneous photography was a couple of decades old and increasingly able to capture natural lighting effects in landscape studies. But the movement of water – as well as some other natural phenomena like smoke rising or leaves blowing in the wind – was one thing that motion pictures could achieve that would convince the photography establishment to take it seriously. Certainly still photography had the edge on quality. There were constant complaints in the first few years of film projections that the pictures were indistinct, flickery or unsteady. But however imperfect, moving pictures offered a new sense of wonder in the way people looked at the world. It was now possible to copy time, albeit in small segments, to see people 'in the flesh' without meeting them, to see places in great detail without travelling to them, to enjoy the whole of the world from your chair. It was the beginning of a new method of documenting events and practices, and particularly the delights of the natural world.

Films of sea waves, rough seas or waterfalls began to proliferate, becoming a surprisingly enduring mini-genre. Many examples have survived, such as the beautiful *A Sea Cave Near Lisbon*, filmed by Henry Short for Robert Paul in 1896, in which Portugal's famous Boca di Inferno (mouth of Hell) frames the waves swirling and smashing against the rocks. Other film producers followed: Bamforth, Prestwich, Esmé Collings and the amateur William Henry Youdale, the Warwick Trading Company and Mitchell and Kenyon. The Lumière brothers got in on the act in April 1896. Several surviving films of this type can't be matched to a filmmaker. Without any recognisable features in the landscape we can only identify films using accumulated knowledge of camera types, frame and perforation shapes and formats. The origin of some of these films will probably remain a mystery.

The genre soon extended to scenes such as the wakes of ships at sea (*Churned Waters*, Warwick Trading Company, 1899) and views of children playing on beaches. These were very much in the picturesque mode. For example, Lumière's *Enfants pêchent des crevettes* (*Children Fishing for Shrimps*), filmed in Britain in July or August 1896 by Alexander Promio, is reminiscent of a popular piece of *belle époque* marketing. Perhaps the cameraman was merely attracted to the group on the beach by its similarity to the familiar image, but even in the most apparently natural of films we have to question the degree of staging of the human figures. Waves, of course can't be staged. The speed of the movement of water is a constant – we instinctively know if it's too fast or too slow – it is a standard against which we can measure the 'realness' of a film. Arthur Cheetham's charming views, such as *Children Playing on the Beach at Rhyl* (1898), identifiable from the pier on the horizon, capture some of that feeling of 'realness'. Nature, children and animals have a timeless quality that adults seem to lack, as Mariann Lewinsky, noted in response to a screening of Lumière films from 1896:

> A flag flying, for example, crosses over easily and reaches the present, so does the play of light and shadow on a Boston tramway, and while a Tsar or a dowager Empress of Russia remains bound to the past, animals and children are free, timeless. The uncanny magic of time in these very early films is overwhelming. How is it possible that we should be permitted to see the past, in 50 second glimpses?[72]

Launch of the Worthing Lifeboat – Coming Ashore (Biograph, 1898).

Cecil Hepworth was still making films of breakers on a rocky shore as late as 1903, so clearly these films had a strong appeal that outlasted their initial novelty. Miriam Hansen suggests that in the early days,

> If the traditional arts required... concentration upon a singular object or event, the variety format provided a short-term but incessant sensorial stimulation, a mobilization of the viewer's attention through a discontinuous series of attractions, shocks and surprises.[73]

It seems that sensory overload is not just a modern phenomenon. Perhaps the more relaxing images like sea waves offered some relief from the hyper-kinetics of other genres.

The venues in which early films shows were exhibited and the pre-existing forms of 'picture-going' did much to shape the subjects filmmakers chose to film and the way they presented them. Attention still had to be grabbed, and entertainment, news and spectacle delivered, but even in Victorian entertainment spaces there was also an emphasis to the 'improving' nature of the performance. Films even imitated fine art, with a trend for films based on 'living pictures' or *tableaux vivants*, or directly from famous paintings themselves. There are many surviving examples, although only one from Britain in the Victorian era: *The Spirit of his Forefathers* (1900), by the British Mutoscope & Biograph Company. This advertising film for Dewar's Whisky, based on an 1894 painting by Matthew B. Hewerdine, features portraits of a Scottish laird's ancestors climbing out of their frames to drink a toast with him. Art historian Lynda Nead observes in this film, and in *The Haunted Picture Gallery*, a lost G. A. Smith film, the coincidence of the aesthetic relationship between the frames of paintings in a gallery and the individual frames of the film print

> A space for pictures and for ghosts, the gallery is also for endless pacing watched by portraits of generations of the dead… How apt that the shadows cast on the ceiling by the windows and tapestried walls look like a strip of film, with intermittent, spaced-out picture frames, separated by short intervals of blank darkness. Set this sequence in motion and the enchantment begins; the pictures come to life and the ghosts haunt the gallery.[74]

While actualities are abundant, films of this era based on scientific subjects are rare, and of those only a handful survive. But few as they are, they do demonstrate links between film and the world of Victorian popular science. There were two essential approaches to films focusing on nature – aesthetic and documentary. Colour applied by hand, on such films as *Conway Castle: Panoramic View of Conway on the L. & N.W Railway* (1898) was an aesthetic choice. The 'rough sea' films, and other highly composed landscape films, such as *Launch of the Worthing Lifeboat: Coming Ashore* (1898) or the *Battle of Spion Kop* (1900), seem to reflect a visual style inherited from fine art via photography, drawing on Victorian notions of the sublime and picturesque. This type of composition, achieving defined foreground, middle ground and background elements with lenses that could register a high degree of depth-of-field with everything in focus, is one of the most attractive features of these films.

Films of animals, such as the Biograph's *Pelicans in the Zoo* (1898), combine both the aesthetic and the documentary approach and display a kinship with the 'chronophotographs' of Eadweard Muybridge and Étienne-Jules Marey. The close camera position, as if to enable detailed observation of the birds, is balanced by the natural beauty of the image. More straightforwardly documentary in feel is G. A. Smith's *Spiders on a Web* (1900), which frames its close-up image in a circular mask as if it were taken using a microscope (audiences interested in natural history would have been familiar with images of this type from lantern lectures). The film industry would, in the early 1900s, take up the painstaking work of documenting flora and fauna for the public's edification. Britain has documented natural history subjects on film since the Victorian era with great continuity, benefiting from the widespread amateur interest cultivated by the Victorian educationalists.

Worldwide, film was increasingly being taken up as a serious scientific tool. Experiments in micro-cinematography emerged in many countries, notably in the US by the physician Robert Lincoln Watkins, while filmed

Pelicans at the Zoo (Biograph, 1899).

G. A. Smith's *Spiders on a Web* (1900).

medical studies were released in Romania and France. At a meeting of the Glasgow Philosophical Society in April 1897, Dr John Macintyre demonstrated the first X-Ray cinematography with a film known as *Dr Macintyre's X-Ray Film* (1897). The *British Journal of Photography*'s report of its filming at the Royal Society, includes very useful details of its complex filming method:

> Controlling the motions of a frog's limbs by mechanical means, he illuminated them by a Crookes' tube, actuated by a ten-inch spark coil. He then covered the instrument with lead foil, presumably removing the lens, and substituting for it a lead diaphragm, with small aperture. Then illuminating the tube, and setting the kinematograph, supplied with thirty-five feet of film, in motion, he obtained a series of views of the skeleton, which, placed in the instrument, enabled him to show to a large audience the actual movements of the bones of the limbs.[75]

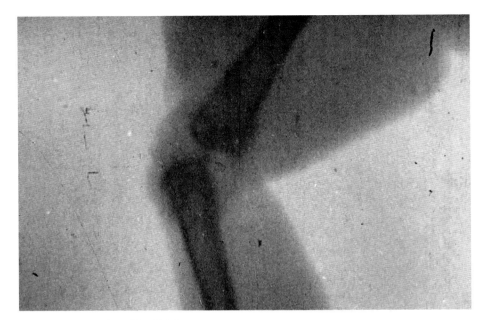

Dr. Macintyre's X-Ray Film (1897).

After the first demonstration of the 'Roentgen ray' in November 1895, a kind of X-ray fever swept the land. Showmen toured with X-ray demonstrations, revealing the inner workings of the body as a modern wonder. G. A. Smith rushed out a spoof comic sketch, *X-Rays*, in October 1897 starring Laura Bayley and Tom Green, using very basic props with skeletons painted on body stockings and a cardboard X-ray machine. It has been a comic trope ever since.

In 1900 filmmakers made their most ambitious attempt to progress science by filming for the first time a full solar eclipse, to take place on 28 May. This would be an extremely expensive and difficult photographic feat, requiring custom-built equipment and perfect weather conditions. Cecil Hepworth filmed it from Algiers but his effort was unsuccessful and doesn't survive. But J. N. Maskelyne, a keen astronomer, magician and part owner with his father Nevil Maskelyne of the famous Egyptian Hall Theatre, pulled off a coup by successfully taking a film of the eclipse from North Carolina, which he screened at the theatre in Piccadilly on many occasions. *The Era* judged the Egyptian Hall's programme '(t)he finest and most exclusive series

J. N. Maskelyne's *Solar Eclipse* (1900). Courtesy of the Royal Astronomical Society.

of Animated Photographs ever exhibited', hailing the eclipse film as 'the first occasion that animated photography has been successfully employed in astronomical research'.[76] A fragment of the film survives at the Royal Astronomical Society, where it was also screened. This shows moments from the eclipse at totality, with the corona and the phenomenon of the Bailey's beads or 'diamond ring' effect visible.

Maskelyne's film highlights the porous border between art, entertainment and science in the late-Victorian period. Scientific subjects could be exhibited in highly respectable scientific institutions as well as in the context of magic, spiritualist and other very non-scientific demonstrations. Like many successful 'magicians', the Maskelynes typically formulated their shows as if examining supernatural phenomena in a scientific way. Here they did the opposite, showing a film genuinely made for scientific reasons, as a piece of mystical entertainment. For now, this kind of boundary crossing would remain a common feature of early film exhibition, tying even the most scientific of films to novelty and spectacle.

Close-up: The Victorian Commercial

One type of Victorian film is instantly recognisable to us today: the 30-second advertisement.

When Robert Paul floated his company in 1897 he expected that making films for commercial clients would earn as much as £15,000 profit, about half its total income. His 'animated advertisements' would be 'adaptable to any trade and showing processes of manufacture or use of any commodity in life-like operation.' But the activity never got going, and after a flurry of interest, film ads more or less disappeared.

The first advertising films emerged almost simultaneously in 1897/98 in New York, Paris and London. In London, Charles Goodwin Norton's *Vinolia Soap* (1898) featured women factory workers packing boxes in front of a huge branded banner. In Paris, Felix Mesguich and Georges Méliès filmed adverts for luxury products which were projected onto large screens in busy thoroughfares. There were similar exhibitions in New York's Union Square around the same time. Edison produced an ad for *Admiral Cigarettes* (1897), while in 1899, the dynamic Tommy Dewar, of Dewar's Scotch, commissioned the International Film Company to turn a celebrated Dewar's poster into a filmed advertisement. In it, a Scottish Laird relaxes with a dram surrounded by framed portraits of his ancestors, at which point the figures begin to climb out of their

The Spirit of his Forefathers (left) and *Rudge and Whitworth, Britain's Best Bicycle* (both British Biograph, 1899).

frames and join their descendent in a toast to the Queen. A surviving fragment of the film, *Whisky of His Ancestors*, shows them all dancing a lively reel.

This same scene was filmed again in 1900 in London by the British Mutoscope and Biograph Company, as *The Spirit of his Forefathers*. The Dewar's name is again clear to see at the top of the frame but in another copy held at the BFI National Archive this has been cropped off so that the film could be repurposed as a comic subject.

Other British ads, all from Biograph, were trials for the 'Advertising Mutoscope', a multi-person viewer for commercial use. The only survivor, *Rudge and Whitworth, Britain's Best Bicycle* (c. 1901), is a model of clarity. A young man arrives by bike, puffing and wheezing, to where a smiling young lady is standing. Evidently his machine is too heavy. Hers, on the other hand, is light. Pointing to the poster behind her, she mouths, 'Rudge and Whitworth, Britain's – best – bicycle'. He picks up her bike and acknowledges it is lighter. The prominently displayed brand name, use of attractive models and clear demonstration of the product's utility are all techniques familiar to advertisers and audiences today.

It's clear from the rare surviving advertising films that filmmakers knew how to adapt existing advertising concepts for moving pictures, and had a feel for how audiences would respond. But paying customers wouldn't tolerate them within the ordinary film show. Around 1901, Biograph issued a booklet, 'Picturing Ideas', intended to interest salesmen in portable Mutoscopes":

> *Does Advertising Pay?* That depends on the cleverness with which it is done... The Chief feature in a *good* advertisement is the prominent position it occupies in a paper, book or on a hoarding. In the Mutoscope *your* advertisement *alone* is brought before the eye. It is not crowded together with others more attractive in character or more elaborately displayed.*

But the intended client base for high-end products and the eventual audience for Mutoscopes proved a poor fit. Film advertising would have to wait for the arrival of the cinema, with its longer programme and captive audience.

---

*   Quoted in Richard Brown and Barry Anthony, *A Victorian Film Enterprise: The History of the British Mutoscope and Biograph Company 1897–1915*, p52 and appendix 3.

8 DANCING ON THE CEILING: TRICK FILMS

A magician entertains a group of guests around the table in a Victorian parlour. He makes a top hat rise through the air and then, with a magic pass, vanishes. At that moment, the guests find themselves upside down on the ceiling, where they enjoy the novel sensation by frolicking about. This is *Upside Down, or the Human Flies*, featuring magician Walter Booth, made at Robert Paul's studio in New Southgate, London, in 1899. The trick is ingenious: by shooting the scene against a painted 'parlour' backdrop with real furniture in the foreground, it was necessary only to invert the set and to film the actors rolling about as if on the ceiling, then to print the film upside down. It's one of the best examples of this most popular and enchanting form of early fiction film. Trick films are a fascinating genre, borrowing from other Victorian entertainments and adding their own cinematographic twist. Filmmakers delighted in the opportunity to demonstrate that moving pictures could perform 'magic' tricks that would be difficult or, like Booth's 'human flies' routine, impossible to recreate in a theatre.

At the turn of the century, the popular theatre, with its lavish productions and large casts, dancing and singing, colourful costumes and fantastical scenes, was generally considered the acme of mass entertainment. There were musical revues, Christmas pantomimes and thrilling melodramas, as well as variety programmes competing for attention using ever-more-bizarre novelty acts. These often relied on complex staging, lighting and mechanics to deliver spectacle and illusions. More than the 'highbrow' arts of literature

Upside Down, or the Human Flies (Walter Booth for R. W. Paul, 1899).

or the 'legitimate' theatre, it was *this* array of mass-appeal entertainments that early film imitated. Going to one of these shows would have been a rare treat for many people and a distant aspiration for others, so a short film that satisfied the desire for any part of the experience of such an entertainment would have been a considerable draw. Filmmakers tried to incorporate the most compelling elements of popular theatre, above all, magical effects. With the new technology of moving photography, using 'stop and substitute' (to 'disappear' and replace people or objects), smoke effects, matte work and reversing, they could create new tricks for use within the theatre show, or mimic traditional stagecraft and the language and aesthetic of popular theatre within their films.

Magicians and magic acts regularly appeared in the music halls, and magic and trickery were principal attractions of many popular stage productions. Magic had its own specialist theatre, in one of the oldest

Sam Dalton in James Williamson's *The Magic Extinguisher* (1901).

entertainment establishments in the capital, the legendary Maskelyne and Cooke's Egyptian Hall in Piccadilly, which adopted film early on as a 'turn' within its multi-act show. It's striking how many early filmmakers and showmen had worked in magic theatres or were performing illusionists: France could count Georges Méliès, Félicien Trewey and Gaston Velle, while Britain had not just Walter Booth, who did many of the best trick films for Robert Paul, but also Carl Hertz, G. A. Smith, John Nevil Maskelyne and David Devant. All had worked as illusionists before trying their hand at film, and some of them knew each other well.

The conjuror David Devant was a pivotal figure. An early adopter of cinematography, he was the first man to buy a Theatrograph projector from Robert Paul, and soon began showing film regularly at the Egyptian Hall. Devant had known Georges Méliès since the 1880s (when the latter had made a long stay in London), learning at Maskelyne and Cooke's before acquiring the Théâtre Robert Houdin, a similar establishment in Paris. When

Méliès was unable to buy a Lumière Cinematograph in Paris, he turned to Devant, who sold him equipment made by Paul. Later, Devant made regular visits to Paris, buying films from Méliès to show in Britain. As a performer, he was filmed by Méliès in *D. Devant Prestidigitation* (1897), and several times by Paul, though of the latter films only some fragments of *The Egg Laying Man* and *The Mysterious Rabbit* (both 1896) survive in a Filoscope version.[77] Paul also filmed John Nevil Maskelyne doing his plate-spinning act.

Félicien Trewey was already familiar to London music hall audiences as a performer of 'shadowgraphy' (hand shadows), among other acts, when he was appointed by Lumière in early 1896 to oversee the press show of the Cinematograph in Regent Street and the long-running show at the Empire Leicester Square. Trewey himself formed part of the entertainment in films by the Lumière Brothers, plate spinning and performing a hat transformation act.

These were the men who brought the magic into films. The magicians, by necessity, had excellent mechanical skills. Many of their illusions required specially-built sets, perspective painting and moving parts. They were already in the business of showing illusions and mechanical novelties, as well as performing sleight of hand and other physical tricks. Understandably perhaps, the magicians-turned-filmmakers always included the figure of the magician in their trick films. This tells us that the intention was to reference the stage version of the act as much as to show the illusion itself. The more elaborate stage tricks required purpose-built sets or, as with the popular Victorian 'phantasmagoria' shows, the projection of ghostly apparitions through a semi-transparent screen or on to clouds of smoke. The fearsome finale consisted of the apparition coming closer and closer towards the audience – the very device used to alarm the spectator in early film – and seems to have been used as the ending to several supernaturally-themed trick films, although these endings are often missing from surviving film prints.

Stage magicians were often experienced projectionists even before film arrived on the scene. Many used magic lanterns for shadowgraphy or acts incorporating supernatural elements on screens or backdrops, and they would have learned techniques from lantern shows, including pans, zooms and dissolves, as well as the practice of narrativising their tricks by putting scenes together. They could also draw upon a repertoire of scenarios passed down by earlier generations of magicians and lanternists that might translate well to moving pictures. Classics such as the 'mango tree trick' from India – in which a seed appears to grow unaided from the ground and bear fruit – could be recreated on film, as in Paul's (sadly lost) *Hindoo Jugglers* (1900).

Some popular stage shows, such as pantomimes and melodramas, incorporated film as a trick or novelty interlude. As early as 1896 Paul used some of his films in a pantomime in Brighton, 'Babes in the Wood and Robin Hood'. The films were written into the narrative as the magical vision of the character Father Time, as a contemporary review explains:

> Father Time makes it convenient to take his numerous company to his cave, where he shows them the latest wonders in animated photography, in other words the "Theatrograph", the series of views and incidents affording unbounded pleasure and winning enthusiastic recognition.[78]

A fad around 1899 for integrating film into pantomime or melodrama proved shortlived, although it would resurface now and again (as it still does). A few of these *'entr'acte'* (literally, 'between acts') films have survived. *Mr Moon* (1900) was commissioned from Mitchell and Kenyon by Perci Honri, a virtuoso concertina player and producer of musical revues. Using dark velvet, Honri's face is masked to form a moon face, which makes a series of grimaces in the manner of a 'facial' film. A small, banjolele-playing body is revealed, with the performer's fingers poking through the cloth for legs. After finishing his tune ('Mr Moon' was a song in Honri's show), the moon face sinks lower and lower until it 'sets' below the frame. We don't know exactly how this was incorporated into the music performance, but we know that a later Honri film, *Quick Change Act* (1908), was used to cover a quick costume change between scenes in the show 'Concordia'. It shows Honri changing his costume – exactly what was happening simultaneously off-stage. Perhaps *Mr Moon* performed a similar function, or was simply a gimmick using the new medium.

In G. A. Smith's similar *Miss Bayley* (also known as *Lettie Limelight in her Lair*, 1900) Eva Bayley (sister of Laura) sits backstage, doing her coiffure and gurning at the camera. But if this is, as seems likely, another *entr'acte* film, we have no evidence to confirm it. We do know, however, that in 1899 the British

Mitchell and Kenyon for Percy Honri, here as *Mr Moon* (1901).

Mutoscope and Biograph Company filmed a scene for a Drury Lane melodrama, 'Hearts are Trumps'. In the final act the villain, Lord Beresford, who is caught flirting with a music hall dancer, is seen by his fiancée on screen at a music hall film show. An illustration in *The Sketch* shows the roll-down screen above the stage ready for use.[79] Other popular shows used film to visualise a scene that might otherwise be difficult or impossible to stage, as in 'The Great Millionaire' – a 'monstrous Drury Lane melodrama', according to the *Tatler*'s reviewer, who mocked its spectacular elements including 'a (dustless) motor race along cinematographed road in the moonlight: the vanishing of the motor number one (pursued by motor number two) over a precipice.'[80]

The vogue for spectacular filmed sections in stage plays seems to have followed the motor cars over the precipice, but it reveals producers' willingness to try anything once. It might even explain a mystery surrounding a 'facial' film known as *Herbert Campbell as Little Bobby*, made by Biograph in 1899, when the music hall star was performing as the baby giant in the pantomime 'Jack and the Beanstalk'. Might the film have been intended to be incorporated into the production? There's nothing in the pantomime 'book' to indicate this, and no known evidence that the film was ever shown at the Palace Theatre (where Biograph showed their films), or anywhere else. Given the film's quality and the celebrity of its star, though, it must surely have had *some* purpose.

Conversely, some films plundered the comic 'business' and narratives of pantomime as scenarios for their tricks, as in James Williamson's *Clown Barber* (1898), which survives only in the catalogue description:

> Gentleman enters barber's shop, knocks and takes a seat. Clown enters, to evident consternation of customer, dances round, and proceeds with the shaving, using a large bowl and brush; lathers him, and then producing a huge razor, commences to shave, but the gentleman becoming alarmed, and rather restive, cuts his head off, and finishes the operation at the sideboard; puts the head on again; customer gets up, expresses his entire satisfaction at the success of the operation, pays and departs.[81]

Barbershop routines were perennial in pantomime and circus clowning and went back as far as the early 19th century.[82] Williamson's film must have used a stop-and-substitute technique, best known today from Georges Méliès films such as *Un homme de têtes* (1898), in which Méliès himself detaches his head and places it on a table, repeating the action until he is surrounded by four 'magically' disembodied heads.

Many early filmmakers, such as Robert Paul, James Williamson and G. A. Smith, were accomplished mechanics, engineers or photographers with a strong grounding in science. They were well-equipped to adapt lantern stories and other visual material from the stage for trick film. A 1912 description of Robert Paul's New Southgate studio shows how conceptually close his thinking was to contemporary stage mechanics:

> It was a combination of a theatre with an ordinary photographic studio utilised for portraiture, in a commodious lofty hall, with a proscenium opening measuring 18 feet in width by 13 feet in height. The stage level was

about 8 feet above the ground, the under part being available for working effects from below, such as bridges, stage traps, and other artifices of the playhouse... A special platform, running on a wheeled carriage and track, the deck of which was level with the floor of the stage, was laid opposite and at right angles to the proscenium opening, to accommodate the camera and operator. Looking into the studio from this point, one saw a familiar theatre stage, with wings, flies, and other facilities... [83]

One film using these resources, though lost, is well described in the Warwick Trading Company's 1897–98 catalogue. *The Mystic Chamber* featured four clowns who chase each other 'through the fireplace, down the chimney, over and between furniture, closets, and wall panels, in fact they vanish and appear in the most unexpected places.' This sounds typical of on-stage chases during the harlequinade, which usually involved different types of trap door set in the walls and the floor, through which the clowns jumped or rolled or were propelled with some force. This kind of scenario adapted well to a haunted house type of story, full of trick walls and props that move as if possessed.

The same Warwick list continues with 'English Films', all by George Albert Smith and badged G. A. S. films, befitting their light-hearted nature. This series, made in 1898, serves as a good summary of the techniques film-makers had developed by that time. Some are photographic 'films within films', used to indicate visions or reveries, as in *Cinderella*, in which the heroine imagines herself dancing with the prince in an insert in the top part of the frame, much like a cartoon thought bubble. *Photographing a Ghost* uses double exposure for the phantom effect, as a mischievous spirit evades the attempts of the photographer to capture it on film until, with a nod to the stage tricks from which it derived, it disappears through the floor. In a stage version, this would have been done with a trap door, known as a 'vampire trap'. Another celebrated trap door effect, the 'Corsican trap', takes its name from 'The Corsican Brothers', well-known melodrama in which a twin is visited by the ghost of his murdered brother – a scene realised with a specially-designed trap door effect allowing the ghost to rise gradually out of the floor. In the (lost) film adaptation, the ghost would again have been achieved by double exposure, while the vision of the murder, in a duel in the snow, would have been done with a filmed scene inserted in vignette.

R. W. Paul's *The Haunted Curiosity Shop* (1900).

Smith's *Faust and Mephistopheles* (1898) employed another stage trick, disguising disappearances and transformations with smoke, as the catalogue describes:

> Mephistopheles appears in a cloud of smoke (fine effects)... Mephistopheles triumphantly waves drinking cup causing it to emit smoke which falls around Faust as he changes to handsome young man.[84]

The Mesmerist (1898) reflected tricks which Smith would have known from his spiritualist days. In it a 'professor' mesmerises a little girl. In another example of superimposition, the girl's spirit rises out of the body, walks around, then falls back into the body.

Trick films became more elaborate by the end of the Victorian era, thanks less to the development of any new technique than to the combination of multiple and more accomplished effects. Robert Paul's catalogue of 1901 lists a few key films as 'Original Trick and Effect Subjects', among them *The Haunted Curiosity Shop* (1900), which combines at breathtaking pace all the trick techniques of the time: superimposition, matte work, stop motion and smoke effects. The shop of the title is stuffed with classic props and characters of a magic theatre: a magical cabinet, floating skulls, gnomes, Egyptian mummies, the bodiless armour of a medieval knight, a lady sawn in half, skeletons and finally a grotesque head which grows larger and larger, 'till it fills the entire picture and appears as though it would swallow the whole audience.'[85] Frustratingly, once again the surviving print is missing its exciting ending. In *Chinese Magic Extraordinary* (1901, lost), a Chinese magician with a collection of Chinoiserie props performs various tricks, including transforming girls into butterflies, before the long sleeves of his robe become giant bat wings on which he flies towards the audience. In *Cheese Mites; Or, Lilliputians in a London Restaurant* (1901), Paul uses a near-seamless matte shot (superimposition on a black background) to insert tiny people into a restaurant scene in which a tipsy diner 'sees' mites emerging from his cheese.

Cheese Mites; Or, Lilliputians in a London Restaurant (Walter Booth for R. W. Paul, 1901).

Paul's catalogue separates out a little group of 'Sensational Films', which focus on the drama but rely on an inventive combination of built scenery with trick shots. *Diving for Treasure* (1900) features a daring undersea escape by famous criminal Jack Sheppard (filmed through an aquarium with real fish), while *Plucked from the Burning* (1900), shows a mother and child rescued from a blaze. In *A Railway Collision* (1900), two trains smash together in an elaborate if obvious model shot, but the catalogue description emphasises the story, not the cleverness of the trick work. An early version of 'The Last Days of Pompeii' (1900) follows the staging of theatrical versions in which the trick set, formed of the pillars of the Roman house with Vesuvius erupting in the distant background, collapses dramatically.

One early trick that was purely photographic and owed nothing to the live stage was the briefly-popular reversing film. A few magic lantern and toy tricks implied reversing, but nothing that could match the effect used in surviving films by Cecil Hepworth, G. A. Smith and James Williamson. Hepworth's *The Bathers* (1900) reversed a shot of men plunging into water

James Williamson's *The Puzzled Bather and His Animated Clothes* (1901).

Cecil Hepworth's *The House that Jack Built* (1900).

to make them leap back out again. Williamson's more elaborate *The Puzzled Bather and His Animated Clothes* (1901) employed a stop-motion trick to present a would-be bather who finds that each outfit he removes is magically replaced by another. Finally he gives up and jumps in fully clothed, at which point the picture is reversed, ejecting him from the water, now unexpectedly wearing his swimming costume. Smith uses a similar effect in *The House that Jack Built* (1900): a small girl is building a house when her young brother appears and mischievously knocks it down, bit by bit. After a title card saying only 'REVERSED', the film is run backwards and he appears by magic to build the house again. This, incidentally, is one of the earliest surviving examples of intertitles, which were not extensively used till after the Victorian era.[86]

Cecil Hepworth's *Explosion of a Motor Car* (1900).

Hepworth specialised around this time in trick films involving motorcars. The delightfully gruesome *Explosion of a Motor Car* (1900) uses an impressive smoke bomb explosion as the car blows its passengers to smithereens, and stop and substitution for the ensuing rain of limbs. In *How it Feels to be Run Over* (1900), the car drives straight at the camera and, as if it has collided with the audience, is replaced by a succession of drawn exclamation and question marks (like the asterisks or birds circling used in cartoons to indicate concussion) followed by the words 'Oh! – Mother – will – be – pleased', the exact meaning of which remains mysterious.[87] Hepworth continued his favoured motoring theme long into the 1900s, with films like *The Dog Outwits the Kidnappers* (1908) in which a dog (Blair, star of Hepworth's celebrated *Rescued by Rover*, 1905) manages to drive a car to rescue the family baby.

The Eccentric Dancer (1900), a lost Hepworth film described in his memoirs,[88] uses another trick effect, over-cranking the camera to create slow motion. We do have *Indian Chief and the Seidlitz Powder* (1901), in which

Hepworth uses this technique to show the title character floating as if inflated with gas produced by too much stomach powder.

We can see clearly with these films the overlap between comedy and trick film, from the kind of film in which the magician 'performed' to the camera in imitation of stage acts to those that integrated their effects into a comic narrative. But the techniques developed for the trick film would also fuel the rise of fantasy film as a distinct form – one in which French filmmakers in particular would excel. Méliès' hugely popular and influential *Le Voyage dans la lune* (*Trip to the Moon*, 1902) spawned a decade of films celebrating the colour, fantasy and spectacle of popular theatre, which built on early filmmakers' attempts to emulate features of those productions. Augustus Harris and Alf Collins, the theatrical impresarios who had mounted those Drury Lane sensation plays and pantomimes, had faced criticism as cast numbers multiplied and ever more elaborate special effects dominated – to the point, it was said, that 'Laughter is sacrificed to scenery'.[89] Narrative, too, could get lost in the mêlée – a complaint that would much later, in the era of special effects blockbusters, be directed at film. This, though, had been the priority of fantasy films from the very start, as Méliès confirmed in a 1961 interview:

> As for the scenario, the 'fable' or 'tale', I only consider it at the end... I use it merely as a pretext for the 'stage effects', the 'tricks', or for a nicely arranged tableau.[90]

This emphasis is really the key distinction between early trick film and the narrative fiction film of the cinema to come.

9 LARKING ABOUT: COMEDY

The first filmgoers naturally thought of moving pictures as a photograph that moves. But Victorian photographs famously tend to be stiff and sombre: long exposure times meant sitters had to pose unsmiling, and even when 'instantaneous' photography took off in the 1880s, photographs were relatively costly and typically imitated painted portraits. So it's easy to see the appeal, for 1890s audiences, of humorous films, such as those showing facial expressions in extravagant movement. Victorian audiences might have seen transforming expressions and grimaces before, in magic lantern slides or in illustrations and cartoons, but real faces, particularly in close-up, have a quite different effect.

The simplest comic films or 'facials', as film historians call them, show a character making faces in reaction to a situation, as in G. A. Smith's *Old Man Drinking a Glass of Beer* (1897) or *A Dull Razor* (1900), in which the actor Tom Green, who specialised in these films, shows, respectively, his delight and discomfort. In Biograph's *The Fateful Letter* (1898), Ben Nathan's series of expressions allow us to guess the contents of the letter. *Two Old Sports* (1900) presents a double facial, with a pair of stage-door Johnnies leering over the female forms in a Pantomime programme. Some have an element of story; in *Old Maid's Valentine* (1900), an 'old maid' (Eva Bayley) reacts with shocked and coy expressions to a valentine letter sent as a prank. The device is simple and effective, and still gets a reaction from audiences today. It's hard not to smile at *Two Laughing Men* (1900), featuring the filmmaker Walter Gibbons and Harry Smith, or be rendered queasy by *Herbert Campbell as Little Bobby* (1899) gorging on a plate of revolting gloop.

Eva Bayley in G. A. Smith's *Old Maid's Valentine* (1900).

The facial film also added something to other Victorian entertainments. A performer in a stage farce, comic sketch or pantomime might employ similarly exaggerated facial expressions, but audiences could only enjoy them at a distance. A film audience, however, could revel in every detail – and all the better if it was a celebrity performer such as Herbert Campbell. Early film catalogues frequently call attention to the clarity and realism of the expressions, as in this description of a (lost) Hepworth film, *Comic Grimacer*:

> A human face shown the full size of the screen is always a comic and interesting sight, and when the face is of the 'India-rubber' variety, and the owner can pull it about and distort it into frightful and hideous knots, the pictures result is bound to be interesting and laughable.[91]

This type of film doesn't survive more than a few years beyond the Victorian era, although a vestige of them can be seen in comedies of the 1910s, in the 'emblematic shot': a close-up of a performer at the start or end of a film, often involving comic facial expressions and intended either to establish the actor with their character, or as a kind of curtain call..

If facials were conceptually equivalent to a portrait or photograph, strip cartoons made from a sequence of three or four pictures translated well into short comic scenes. Some were simple stories of cause and effect, as in a popular sub-genre in which a courting couple are interrupted on a park bench. Others were character-led, with protagonists such as opportunistic tramp Weary Willie, or Ally Sloper, a W. C. Fields-style drunken idler. In *The Barber Saw the Joke* (c. 1900) we see one of the funny papers from which this inspiration came, *Ally Sloper's Half Holiday*. Cartoon strips were effectively used as storyboards for short films. Magic lantern stories likewise adapted well. G. A. Smith's *The Miller and the Sweep* (1897), one of the best early British comedies, was a loose adaptation of a lanternist's favourite. It's an example of a 'black and white' comedy, relying on this simple binary for its humour: passing a windmill, a miller with a bag of flour accidentally bumps

The Barber Saw the Joke (British Biograph, 1900).

G. A. Smith's *The Miller and the Sweep* (1897).

into a sweep carrying a bag of soot. The result is an entertaining slapstick fight in which the miller becomes covered with soot and the sweep with flour. The film even has a little coda, as a crowd of onlookers arrives to chase the pair away, prefiguring the chase comedy that would become so popular in the 1900s. Another 'black and white' comedy survives in James Williamson's *Washing the Sweep* (1898), in which a sweep brushing past some newly laundered white sheets is set upon by the laundresses and forcibly scrubbed in a washing trough. An archetypal 'bit with a dog' adds nicely to the comic chaos (as Williamson's catalogue description puts it, 'a terrier assists in a very natural manner').[92] Even if their presence was carefully staged, live animals introduced a pleasingly unpredictable element, reminiscent of the anarchic clowning and chases of the pantomime.

Not all stage comedy translated so easily into film. Many acts were primarily verbal, relying on songs and patter. Films principally consisted of 'low comedy', hinging on buffoonery or lasciviousness. Clown acts, which were done in 'dumb show' adapted well, while other parts of the pantomime tradition can be detected in early films. This may well explain the number of comedies that feature men in drag, for example *Landing an Old Lady from a Small Boat or Lady and the Boat* (1899). In this comedy by Haydon and Urry, two men attempt clumsily to help an old lady (a man in drag) disembark from a small rowing boat, eventually dropping her in the water. So extraordinarily popular was it that exhibitor EG Turner bought 80 prints for distribution.

The comedy of exaggeration can also be seen in films featuring characters from the harlequinade. This was a self-contained scene within a pantomime, in which the protagonists are transformed into a handful of stock characters: Harlequin and Columbine (the young lovers), Clown and Pantaloon (a mischief maker and an old man, sometimes Columbine's father) and often a comedy policeman, a rather gormless authority figure who the others would bambooozle. Victorian audiences would have been familiar with these characters, from pantomime and other entertainments such as toy theatres and Punch and Judy puppet shows. Hepworth's *Clown and Police* (1900) recreates a typical harlequinade scene using the new techniques of cinematography.[93] It opens with the clown and the old man character about to fire a barrel of gunpowder when a policeman appears on the scene. The two mischief-makers vanish into thin air; the barrel explodes leaving the

Cecil Hepworth's *Clown and Police* (1900).

policemen in pieces, but the clown and his friend magically re-assemble him and a general mêlée ensues.

Cecil Hepworth repeats this comic device in *Explosion of a Motor Car* (1900), in which a policeman, searching for survivors with a telescope, is showered with body parts and clumsily attempts to reassemble them. Although the severed limbs clearly belong in the safe world of Victorian children's panto, for those new to moving pictures, this grisly joke might be a shock.

Another recurring theme is romance, albeit in a form barely more sophisticated than the perennial drivers of the pantomime plot: old men pursuing young women behind their wives' backs, young couples trying to evade adult interference, and all the comings and goings of soldiers and nursemaids, artists and models, wives, lovers and husbands. Some of these comic sketches are based on stage pieces: Biograph's *He and She* (1898), in which a young wife is furious at her older husband's late return, features actors

Roma T. Roma and Frank Wood recreating their own stage act, while R. W. Paul's similar *Two A.M. or the Husband's Return* (1896) is described in the Alhambra theatre programme for 31st August 1896 as a 'comic scene by Mons. Paul Clerget and Miss Ross Selwicke'. G. A. Smith's *Policeman and the Cook or the Copper in the Copper* (1898), which hasn't survived, was based on the well-known farce 'Area Belle'. In each case the catalogues credit the theatrical source, so there was clearly some advantage to be gained. Britain's first-ever comic drama, Paul's *The Soldier's Courtship* (described in Chapter 1) is a film of this type as early as 1896.

If some of these comedies might seem slightly unsavoury today, they were evidently within the bounds of acceptability drawn by the stage conventions from which they sprang. They ranged from the mildly suggestive, in which the audience is invited behind closed doors to spy on the romantic lives of others, as in *He and She* or *Two AM*, to the straightforwardly slapstick, such as *Lover Kisses Husband* (1900), in which a husband catches his wife kissing a lover on a park bench and substitutes himself while the lover is looking the other way. G. A. Smith's *The Kiss in the Tunnel* (1899) was originally made as a single shot depicting a couple (played by Smith and his wife Laura Bayley) snatching a quick kiss when their train enters a tunnel. Even Victorians couldn't have been too shocked by this scenario, but it does implicate us as spectators of the private or illicit. Later the film was bookended with a 'phantom ride' scene of a train entering and then leaving a tunnel, which added some context, even if it wasn't quite as self-consciously phallic as Hitchcock's famous train tunnel scene in *North By Northwest* (US, 1959).

It's interesting to compare Smith's *The Kiss in the Tunnel* to another version produced, probably soon after, by the Riley Brothers for the Bamforth Company. This has train rides at beginning and end, though in a distant static shot, rather than the more immersive 'phantom ride', in which the audience shares the point of view of the driver. It has a more practical three-dimensional set, but it's in the comedic scenario where the difference is most felt. The man puts down his cigarette and almost launches himself at the woman, kissing her with no preamble. The woman has her back to the audience, which has the effect of objectifying her, whereas in the Smith version Laura Bayley is fully engaged both in the fictional activity and in giving us some sense of character by her performance.

G. A. Smith's *The Kiss in the Tunnel* (1899).

The Smiths were professional performers, who had met as part of J. D. Hunter's company of players working the theatres and piers of the southern coast resorts. They had clearly worked up the scenario to accent flirtatious charm, in contrast to the more brutish Bamforth version. Laura Bayley, probably Britain's most instantly recognisable early screen actor, seems to have had an instinctive feel for the different performance level required for the screen, despite being primarily an actor for the stage. Her performance in this short scene illustrates how skilfully she positions herself in relation to the camera, in order to engage the audience on the other side of the lens. By the time of the very funny *Mary Jane's Mishap* (1903), Bayley's cheeky personality, knowing winks at the camera and large but deliberate gestures mark her out as a gifted screen comedian.

Haydon and Urry's *The Bride's First Night* (1898) takes the voyeurism we see in *The Kiss in the Tunnel* a step further, showing a young bride undressing in a bedroom as her husband watches from behind a screen, getting visibly hot under the collar and wiping his brow with a handkerchief. The film apparently

G. A. Smith's *As Seen Through a Telescope* (1899).

had a sequel, *Twelve Months Later*, which rather hammers the point home.[94] In 1900 G. A. Smith produced *As Seen by a Telescope,* employing the device of the telescope to present the point of view of an older gentlemen ogling a young lady cyclist's ankle, thus validating one of the great Victorian myths, that the sight of an ankle was enough to excite the male sexual appetite. Smith's *Photograph Taken from our Area Window* (1901) is comprised entirely of ankles walking past the basement window across the 'area' of a house (the sunken space between the basement where the servants worked and the outside pavement). The risqué situations implied by, for example, the dropping of a handkerchief by a female and the change in direction of a male, is perhaps all in the voyeur's mind, but of course, it's in the audience's too.

More explicitly risqué is a film called *A Woman Undressing* (1896), attributed to Esmé Collings,[95] in which a woman disrobes to her chemise. Filmed in the open air against a painted flat of a Victorian boudoir, without even the metaphorical fig leaf of a classical setting, it's all quite matter of fact. There is no acting or coquetting, so it's difficult to know if this was shown generally in a slightly naughty, comical sense or just at gentlemen-only events (as a so-called 'smoking party' subject), in which case one might expect it to be a bit more titillating. It has more in common stylistically with the films made for the Mutoscope and similar 'What the Butler Saw' machines, as well as with common still photographs of this type, and would have been offered for sale generally, so perhaps it was left to the exhibitor to decide if it would shock or interest his audience. Elsewhere in Europe, such '*scènes grivoises*' (saucy scenes), were more common.[96] It could be that what we assume about Victorian prudishness is exaggerated; a film in Paul's *Army Life* series showing soldiers naked bathing doesn't seem to have elicited any comment in the contemporary press. Either way, *Woman Undressing* seems to be a one-off; there are no other British films of this kind in the records.

It wasn't long before film comedies began to diverge from their stage or page origins. Paul's *Come Along Do!* (1898), Smith's *Grandma's Reading Glass* (1900) and Williamson's *Are You There?* (1901) all show how the film's novel relationship between viewer and image could be used to comic effect. *Come Along Do!*, named after a stereoscope photograph, begins with an old married couple outside an art gallery (as the signage tells us); a second shot sees the pair inside the gallery, where the old man takes rather too close an interest in a nude classical statue (naked statuary was a favourite 'artistic' theme for film comedy) until the affronted old lady pulls her unsophisticated husband away – establishing the limits of social acceptability. Importantly, in the first example of its kind, the film introduces an establishing scene, which snobbishly illustrating the characters' social class and supplies a shift in location and time between its two scenes. In this we can see a way in which a comic scenario could be fleshed out to build a longer narrative.

By 1901, we find films made up of as many as three separate scenes. In Williamson's *Stop Thief!*, a tramp steals a leg of lamb from a butcher's boy, who turns to chase the thief. In the next part of the chase, the tramp is pursued past some houses, watched by housewives at their doors, before a third scene in which the tramp jumps into a barrel to hide, followed by several dogs drawn by the scent of the meat. The butcher's boy extracts, one by one, the dogs and the thief. In subject matter and staging, this is straight out of the pantomime, which often featured theft from butcher's shops. The geometry of the chase, that is, the direction that the tramp runs on into the scene, would be perfectly acceptable in a stage production, but in film it feels wrong, and not long after this a consensus emerged around the direction of travel in chase scenes.

In G. A. Smith's *Grandma's Reading Glass* (1900), a boy 'sees' a series of objects through a magnifying lens – all shown in close-up, with a circular mask to suggest the view through the glass. Smith effectively 'teaches' us, by repetition, the grammar of seeing the boy and then his point of view. Smith again condenses two shots into one film in *Let Me Dream Again* (1900), framing similar positions of a man and a woman with a small temporal

James Williamson's *Are You There?* (1901).

and spatial shift that changes the meaning: a man (Tom Green) dreams he is drinking and flirting with a young woman (Laura Bayley), then wakes up disgruntled in bed next to his (much older) wife.

In *Are You There?* (1901), Williamson condenses the action by getting *his* two shots in one frame. A man (Williamson's star actor Sam Dalton) enjoys a flirty telephone conversation with his sweetheart. We see them both, separated by a wall (clearly a prop). The girl's father enters, and furiously seizes the phone to discover the identity of her caller; oblivious, the young man continues talking. Subsequently, the father arrives at the young man's house (so time between one action and another has elapsed), and thrashes him with an umbrella. In later films, this might be shown as a split screen. All these films demonstrate some development in terms of playing with the time frame in which the action takes place.

By the end of its first six years, Victorian film comedy had also developed a self-awareness and reflexivity that would recur intermittently in films down the years. Paul's *The Countryman and the Cinematograph* (1901) combines several of the new sensations of moving pictures in one short comedy. A be-smocked yokel is at a city theatre watching a film show. He is at the side of the stage (music halls often had boxes right at the edge) so that we can see him and the film simultaneously. First he has fun mimicking a dancer in the film, then he is alarmed by an oncoming train rushing towards the screen (the sophisticated 1901 audience is, of course, completely unfazed). Finally, he is outraged to discover someone apparently flirting with his milkmaid girlfriend, at which point he tears down the screen to reveal the projectionist behind (this scene is missing in the surviving print). It's a delightful conceit, good enough to be copied soon after by Edwin Porter in the US – a sincere form of flattery. Paul's film may owe something to an 1899 *entr'acte* film used in a stage melodrama called 'Lady of Ostend', in which a man is caught out flirting with a woman on a beach thanks to a cinematograph film shown to the audience of the play-within-the-play.

G. A. Smith's *Snapshotting an Audience* (1900), another film playing with the idea of audience perspective and screen, is sadly lost but, according to *The Era*, it

> shows preparations for taking a group photograph of an imaginary audience which in reality is us, the spectators of the film. He tells various imaginary persons amongst us, to look this way or that, to look pleasant, and so forth. He is, of course, directing his instructions towards the camera, as if it were a member of the audience.[97]

It's almost impossible, then, not to see it as a film about filmmaking, even if the protagonist is not a cinematographer but a photographer – as is the initially unseen character in James Williamson's *The Big Swallow* (1901). This had a scenario to go with it printed in the catalogue. It sets the scene: a gentleman, being harassed by a beach photographer, insists, 'I won't, I won't, be photographed'. In the film, we can see him mouthing these words and thrashing about with his cane. Still protesting, he advances steadily towards the camera until his open mouth fills the screen, at which point we see the photographer, tripod, camera and all, fall into the darkness of his mouth. Finally, we see the man in close-up as he chews and swallows (leaving the audience wondering who was photographing the photographer).

Walter Booth's *Artistic Creation* (1901).

Breaking the fourth wall in this way was not unique to film. Stage drama and comedy had been doing this since ancient times by use of the 'aside', while painting had often spilled over the edge of its frame in *trompe l'oeil* murals. It was natural that film, too, should test its boundaries. In *Artistic Creation* (1901), magician-turned-filmmaker Walter Booth working with Robert Paul, appears as a Pierrot-like character with a magic easel, on which he sketches the head of a young woman. It comes to life, and he lifts the moving head out of the picture and places it on a table. The head demands more body parts and so arms and legs are sketched and attached until she is complete. The Pierrot draws his latter-day Galatea a gift, what every woman apparently wants: a baby. However, our heroine sees what he is up to and flees (a surprisingly modern response on her part). He turns with a real baby in his arms to see she is gone, but what to do with the baby? Finally he breaks the fourth wall and offers it to the audience. The transformations of the drawings into the 'real' woman are so beautifully done, with matting and stop-motion photography, that you can barely see the joins.

What sets this aptly-named film apart is the quality of its conception, imagination and execution: it feels as if it is moving beyond mere trickery and low comedy. Such seamless illusion-making in the service of narrative would draw audiences back to the film show again and again, eager to engage with more complex story and character.

Montage: The Facial

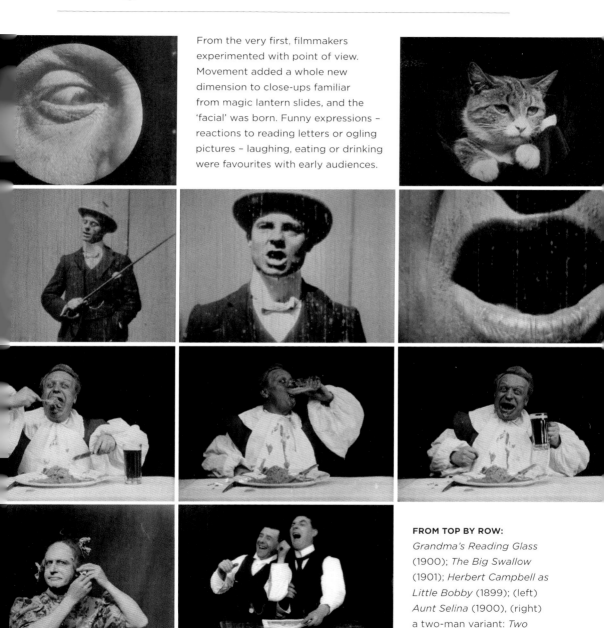

From the very first, filmmakers experimented with point of view. Movement added a whole new dimension to close-ups familiar from magic lantern slides, and the 'facial' was born. Funny expressions – reactions to reading letters or ogling pictures – laughing, eating or drinking were favourites with early audiences.

FROM TOP BY ROW:

Grandma's Reading Glass (1900); *The Big Swallow* (1901); *Herbert Campbell as Little Bobby* (1899); (left) *Aunt Selina* (1900), (right) a two-man variant: *Two Laughing Men* (1900).

10 PLAYS WITHOUT WORDS: DRAMA AND ADAPTATION

The earliest attempts at dramatic storytelling in film around 1898 were frustrating. The short running time of the earliest films made it difficult to tell more than the simplest stories, as Elias Koopman, managing director of the Biograph Company, complained:

> The whole story has to be told in pantomime in less than a minute, without a word of explanation, every movement must be incapable of being misunderstood, and no time be lost, as the film will be exhausted in the three-quarters of a minute allowed.[98]

But it became obvious very early on that minute-long films could be amalgamated, enabling multi-part films to carry slightly more complex narratives, in a similar way to the dramatic tales built around still images by magic lanternists. Other static images, such as book and newspaper illustrations, or 'tableaux vivants' (in which live performers recreated a painting on stage), could provide filmmakers with subjects, while strip cartoons presenting images in a sequence offered an easily-adaptable readymade narrative. Narrative drama films retained this sequential or episodic structure until the very end of our era in 1901, when editing together scenes across different locations or time periods made for a more recognisably 'filmic' storytelling.

Of all of the Victorian-era film forms, the drama has survived in the smallest numbers. But then, the overwhelming majority of films produced between 1895 and 1901 – an average of 85% – were of non-fiction subjects.⁹⁹ For Barry Anthony this was absolutely a function of demand, not expedience:

> The days when a simple street scene drew gasps of amazement soon passed and it was probably easier to film a kissing couple or a thrilling combat than to haul a heavy camera to a predetermined event, secure a reasonable vantage point, then trust that the weather would be sufficiently kind to allow filming. The governing objective of the music hall was to meet audiences' requirements. Had fiction films been more popular than non-fiction films they would assuredly have been provided in greater numbers.¹⁰⁰

Fiction made up some 16% of all films in the period, with 'dramas', as distinct from comedies and trick films, representing less than a fifth of that – in other words, less than 5% of all films produced.¹⁰¹ This might feel surprisingly low: it's tempting to imagine the narrative fiction film in this period as at the beginning of a journey to the cultural and commercial dominance it would

R. W. Paul's *Scrooge; or Marley's Ghost* (1901).

eventually achieve. But it's hard to demonstrate any such ambitions among most of the early filmmakers.

Almost invariably, early commentators imagined film's possibilities in non-fiction terms: to record historical events and people, to advance medicine, to study nature. It's altogether harder to find evidence of the conceptual origins of film drama. Filmmakers were busy supplying the market with what it demanded, within existing entertainment structures, which meant short, and diverse in subject. The pre-existing models for longer drama were – as they had been for some time – the novel, epic poetry, opera and the stage play in its various forms. Each had its own dedicated infrastructure – publishing industry, supply chain, venues – which film still largely lacked. What would impel a maker of animated photographs to consider making a longer narrative?

There was nothing inevitable about the development of the dramatic film; filmmakers might easily have decided the medium wasn't suited to it. But the instinct to replicate other forms of entertainment may supply the clue to how the dramatic film did get started. By far the most profitable period for the popular theatre was the Christmas pantomime season, so it's no surprise that filmmakers tried to exploit this. Adaptations of pantomimes and melodramas seem to have developed as single scenes, strung together to form a longer film in tableaux style, with no scene-to-scene continuity. For these kinds of films we can trace a clear chronology of development over the period.

As we have seen with the coverage of the Diamond Jubilee, as early as 1897 filmmakers began to film multiple shots of potentially profitable footage and soon after were addressing the technical problems of getting longer lengths of celluloid in the camera. Writing in December that year, J. Miller Barr remarked that 'a much longer duration – involving the use of many films – is now practicable.'[102]

By the end of the Victorian era, the catalogues reveal a small number of multi-part fiction films. Some of these were formally similar to the multi-part travel films or series such as *Our Navy* and *Army Life* (which themselves contained dramatised sequences); that is, they were a series of independent scenes that could be shown individually, in groups or all together, according to the exhibitor's preference and budget. 1901 saw the release of Britain's longest fiction film to date: Robert Paul's nine-minute epic *Scrooge, or Marley's Ghost*.

To see what kind of dramatic works were made across the period – whether adaptations of a pre-existing source or 'original' works as we would understand them – it's worth looking at the output of two of the largest producers, the British Biograph company and Robert Paul, who took very different approaches to fiction film. British Biograph produced some adapted fragments of dramas (though not nearly as many as the American company), nearly always featuring named actors. The popular Lewis Waller, who played the villainous Philip Faulconbridge in *King John* (1899), also appeared as the heroic d'Artagnan in *Fencing Contest from the Three Musketeers* (1898). *Duel to the Death* (1898), in which two women fight with swords, was a scene from the contemporary melodrama, 'Women and Wine'.[103] *The Zola Rochefort Duel* (1898) fictionalised a supposed duel between crusading author Emile Zola and a reporter over France's notorious Dreyfus case. In the main, though, British Biograph chose to privilege factual film; it relied heavily on one resident show at the Palace Theatre of Varieties, which became known for its actuality films. The presence on the company's board of newspapermen like Sir George

Herbert Beerbohm Tree in *King John* (Biograph, 1899).

Newnes and Sir Arthur Pearson may have shaped its priorities, but the greater influence on Biograph's indifference to fiction was surely W. K. L. Dickson.

In America, Dickson had designed and built studios – the first in the world – specifically for filming 'acts' and comic scenes from vaudeville for Edison. He built another in the first days of the American Mutoscope and Biograph Company, where he filmed the first multi-scene fiction film, seven scenes of *Rip Van Winkle* (1896), a kind of proto-drama.[104] And he built studios when he arrived in London: one rooftop model somewhere near the Embankment and a fully functioning indoor photographic studio with arc lights in Regent Street around 1900. He had the means and the experience to produce multi-scene films of this type. But he didn't, preferring instead to make adventurous films of important people and events: the Diamond Jubilee, royal coronations, the Boer War, the Pope.

The building of the studios was intended to supply films such as *King John*, four scenes from stage legend Herbert Beerbohm-Tree's new production at Her Majesty's Theatre. Like *Rip Van Winkle*, it was essentially a star vehicle: the actor, not the drama, was the film's main draw. Even the making of the film was publicised; *The Sketch* details the logistical challenge of moving the cast – in full costume – together with props and scenery, down to the Embankment to be filmed by Dickson.[105] On 20th September 1899, the very night of the play's stage premiere, the film scenes were exhibited in Amsterdam, Paris, Brussels, Berlin, Ostend, Glasgow, London, Milan and Vienna. The reasons for making and showing the film were clear; there was no attempt here to 'adapt' Shakespeare's play for the screen. For at least one anonymous reviewer, 'the absence of speech is much more felt than in scenes taken from nature.'[106] That 'absence' might ultimately supply one incentive – commercial as well as aesthetic – for filmmakers to find other ways to get across story in film. A year earlier, a strikingly prescient reviewer in the *Photographic News* had come to a similar conclusion during an evening at Maskelyne and Cooke's Egyptian Hall:

> [We] were interested to observe that not the least appreciated part of the programme was the exhibition of animated photographs.... The reflection occurred to us, that so far little had been done to tell a connected story or narrative by means of animatography, and that probably the idea is capable

of considerable development. Plays without words could in fact be produced by means of the Kinematograph, pending the time when Mr Edison's alleged idea of associating the phonograph with animated photography is realised.[107]

In the meantime, the commercial imperative for Biograph's new studio was less fiction filmmaking than stills photography, celebrity portraiture and the Kinora, a downscaled Mutoscope invented by the Lumière brothers. As the company's AGM heard in 1899:

> We have built a studio on the Thames Embankment ... we shall probably have studios in every large town in the Kingdom where people can go and have their own views taken, and have them represented in Mutoscopes in their own homes.[108]

Dickson carefully segregated the high quality non-fiction product he was making for the high-brow audiences at the Palace Theatre from the slightly coarser fare made for the Mutoscopes, much of it lightly exploitative films of scantily-clad chorus girls and undressing 'brides', mostly imported from the US company. This cheap but lucrative seaside smut paid for those expensive foreign trips to film royalty and popes.

Robert Paul, on the other hand, signalled a clear intention to move into fiction making. In October 1898, in what John Barnes calls 'virtually a manifesto',[109] he declared:

> The cinematograph is played out in the sense that the public no longer rush to see photographs moving; but as a means of entertainment it has never yet been properly exploited. The public have been surfeited with trains, trams, and buses, and beyond a few scenes, whose humour is too French in nature to please English audiences, the capacity of animated pictures for producing breathless sensation, laughter, and tears has hardly been realised.[110]

Paul was certainly more committed to fiction entertainment by 1898, producing an assortment of single-shot dramas that year. *The Arrest of a Deserter* was a pathetic subject in which a man is arrested in the cottage of his old mother, while *A Rescue from Drowning*, issued in two parts, included a daring leap from the riverbank by one of the rescuers. In another pair of dramatic films, *The Sailor's Departure* and *The Sailors Return*, the pathos of the protagonist's long absence is assuaged by his happy return to his wife and new baby. Barnes estimates that Paul produced 41 'made-up films' this year: 30 comedies, seven drama subjects, three described as 'vaudeville' and one fantasy. None of the dramas have survived for us to judge how far they delivered on Paul's promise, but the timing of their production was significant.

Once audiences had grown more used to moving pictures, there does seem to have been a demand for newer, better films. Producers began to appeal to specific audiences, and seasonality became important. Fairgrounds were a growth area after Randall Williams' first film show in 1897, and the great theatres of seaside resorts such as Morecambe, Blackpool and Brighton, could supply huge audiences for film shows in the summer. Catalogues and trade advertisements highlight films specifically produced to amuse families and children at Christmas time. Filmmakers worked hard to exploit the seasonal boost. It was in a Christmas film that we see, in Britain, the longer running time that historians once assumed was the spur for the development of the continuous narrative. In 1901, Paul released his most ambitious film, *Scrooge; or, Marley's Ghost*, with an impressive 12 scenes, each a tableau with dissolves, explanatory title cards and multiple superimpositions. The surviving print, incomplete but still running to over six minutes, has been edited together at some later time; originally the parts would have been separate, adding up to some nine minutes, around 13 times longer than Britain's earliest surviving fiction film, Birt Acres' single-shot *Arrest of a Pickpocket*, made in 1895 for the Paul Kinetoscope.

Paul's multi-scene film was part of a growing trend, possibly influenced by the American production of *Rip Van Winkle* – at least one scene of which was screened at the Palace Theatre in 1897 – and Georges Méliès' purportedly 20-part *Cinderella* (1899). Advertised on the same page of *The Era* as Paul's *Scrooge* was Méliès' *Barbe bleu* (*Bluebeard*, 1901), also in 12 scenes. These fictional films were all representations of stage productions. The immediate inspiration for Méliès' fairytale series came from contemporary stage spectacles, not the published stories. We don't know if he was influenced by G. A. Smith's lost single-shot *Cinderella* (1898), but certainly Smith was early in the field with scenes from famous stage productions using fantastical effects, as with his 1898 releases *The Corsican Brothers*, *Faust and Mephistopheles*,[111] *Cinderella*, *Santa Claus*, *The Mesmerist* and *Photographing a Ghost*.

In December 1900, Smith released a Christmas film, *The Death of Poor Joe*. This single-shot, one-scene film depicts the tragic end of Dickens' poor crossing sweeper (originally 'Jo') from 'Bleak House'. On a snowy night outside a churchyard we see Joe collapse. He is discovered by the nightwatchman, patrolling with his lamp. Fearing being told to 'move on' again, Joe's endurance fails and the watchman comforts him by shining his light to indicate the presence of heaven as he teaches Joe a final prayer. Dickens enthusiasts will know this is unlike Jo's death in the book, but theatre scholars have noted the film's similarity to 'Jo', a popular 1876 stage version by JP Burnett, a vehicle for actress Jennie Lee, who played the 'breeches role' of Jo, with his trademark rags and broom, for 20 years in Britain and America.[112] The casting of a woman, Laura Bayley, as Jo (the watchman is Tom Green), and such stage effects as snow being thrown in from the sides and a follow-spot to indicate the light of the watchman's lamp, offer further evidence that the play was Smith's (or quite likely Bayley's) source of inspiration.

G. A. Smith's *The Death of Poor Joe* (1900).

Paul similarly adapted his *Scrooge* from a one-act play by J. C. Buckstone, with a young Seymour Hicks playing the miser. In his advertisement in *The Era*, Paul says that the film scenes are 'founded on' Dickens' 'A Christmas Carol' and, in another article in the same paper, declares:

> Each scene has been arranged and Animatographed with the greatest care and skill and is carried out on the lines of the play as presented on Tuesday 26th at Sandringham before their Majesties the King and Queen.[113]

Useful descriptions in the press reveal some differences between play and film. Paul's *Scrooge* uses film's advantages to good effect, proceeding from the first set-up, Scrooge's counting house (as in the stage version) to outside his home, where he sees Marley's ghostly face in the door knocker in a nicely-executed trick shot, unachievable on stage. So as with trick films, the exhibition format is the key to understanding adaptation in early films. As Tom Gunning cautions, to approach them 'simply as precursors of later narrative structures is to miss the point. The story simply provides a frame upon which to string a demonstration of the magical possibilities of the cinema.'[114]

The magic lantern show, another Christmas staple, could serve as another model for filmmakers. Much of the language and grammar we associate with film was already present in the lantern shows of fairytales for children and other dramatic stories. The demands of delivering a convincing narrative in 24 slides made lanternists proficient with establishing shots, close-ups and such visual devices as dream clouds, and such techniques, as well as the lanternists' concise storylines, could be adapted more or less wholesale by filmmakers.

A further development just after the end of the Victorian period suggests that these films, whether derived from magic lantern or stage shows, might have provided a kind of template for longer, 'plotted' multi-scene films. So although the Christmas specials by Dickson, Paul and Méliès were made in separate tableaux with no continuity from one scene to the next (and thus didn't advance storytelling technique as film historians would think of it), all were reissued in 1902 or 1903 in compiled versions. In January 1902, the Warwick Trading Co. were offering Méliès' *Barbe bleu* as a 'complete Christmas pantomime' at a total length of 630ft: 'an unequalled attraction for children' in plain and coloured versions.[115] Likewise, Dickson's *Rip van Winkle* was compiled and reissued in the US in 1903. At some point the same happened to Paul's *Scrooge*. We can see how, once these films were shown edited together in sequential order, the idea of the longer story could take hold. Gunning sees in the early chase films dating from about 1903 to 1906 a synthesis of attractions and narrative coming from this kind of film.[116] Hepworth's episodic but sequential *Alice in Wonderland* (1903) is a good example. It was an expensive film, available with colour tints by special order, either in individual scenes or entire.

However, by no means all dramatic films made during the Victorian era were straightforward adaptations of stage productions. There were the inherent dramas of newspaper reports: war, accidents, conflagrations or crime all made good subjects for films. A handful of surviving prints could be considered 'original' dramas. Although a pictorial or theatrical source for some of these may yet be discovered, it's likely they are generic stories of the kind that had long filled the popular press. Several films depict dramatic red-handed 'arrests' of street robbers: Birt Acres' *Arrest of a Pickpocket* (1895) shows a thief wrestled to the ground by a policeman; he escapes, but is pinned down by a passing sailor. In *Footpads* (c. 1896), an elderly gentleman at London's Ludgate Circus is set upon by thieves (a pleasing trick effect, inspired by lantern slides, shows the twinkling electric advertising signs). The lost film *Arrest of a Bookmaker* (1898), which we can with certainty attribute to Paul, has a more complicated plot: an illegal bookmaker unwittingly targets a police officer and is caught in his trap. Crime fiction was perennially popular and, being plot-led, was a good incentive for more elaborate storytelling. We have seen how the comic treatment of a street crime in *Stop Thief!* (1901) was elaborated by James Williamson in three continuous scenes, and by 1903 this was further developed by the Sheffield Photo Company into a fully-fledged, multi-scene crime drama, *A Daring Daylight Robbery*.

Fictional war films, likewise, had natural drama, pathos and the potential for action. Rachael Low and Roger Manvell list several of the types of war film produced to satisfy the tastes of an audience for whom the real war footage couldn't match for excitement the illustrated newspapers such as *Black and White Budget*.[117] Some of these films were clearly generic war tales. Paul's *Bombardment of Mafeking* (1899), for example, was a scene of British soldiers sitting with great *sang froid* round a campfire as shells burst around them

Mitchell and Kenyon's *The Dispatch Bearer* (1900).

(the catalogue mentions that this causes amusement rather than alarm). Although Paul claimed that his films were 'reproductions of incidents', which were 'arranged under the supervision of an experienced military officer from the Front',[118] *Nurses on the Battlefield* (1899) also feels like a generic scene, with doctors and nurses nobly tending British and Boer wounded alike. AC Bromhead of Gaumont confessed that the company's recreation of the *Signing of the Peace at Vereeniging* (1902) was 'ludicrously imaginative', and mistakenly included Lord Roberts, who wasn't actually present at the proceedings.[119]

There were certainly paintings and 'life model' (that is, photographic) lantern slides of similar subjects, such as *Portrait, or the Soldier's Dream of Home* (1900), a story of great pathos expressing the 'thoughts' of a soldier, depicted by a vignette of his wife. But for other stories I have found no specific evidence that any of the surviving films is adapted from artists' drawings of Boer War stories, so we can perhaps assume that filmmakers like Paul and Mitchell and Kenyon, in films like *Dispatch Bearer* and *A Sneaky Boer* (both 1900), made up their own scenarios (the partners had previously issued what they called a 'sensationally dramatic' western-style drama, *Kidnapped by Indians* (1899), which resembles these Boer War scenes). Somewhat ironically, we should perhaps think of these much-maligned so-called 'fake' war films as original dramas.

Stephen Bottomore, writing on the Boer War, quotes from a debate between the war artists and photographers, in which we could include cinematographers. For one side, photography 'absolutely ignores personal valour, or depicts it in so tame a light that the spectator is left stone cold',[120] while another countered, 'the public want the facts and not a melodramatic, drawn version.'[121] The *Church Times* cited one contributor who doubted that many of the 'so-called war films' were even filmed in South Africa, concluding: 'it may be generally assumed that the more thrilling the incident depicted the less amount of truth there is in it.'[122]

Thrilling incidents were usually impractical to stage, as with Paul's *A Railway Collision*, which had to use models to recreate the scene. But the drama surrounding fires could be staged, and such films were immensely popular from the outset. As early as 1894 the Edison Company in America produced a fire drama for the Kinetoscope, *Fire Rescue Scene*. The catalogue description reads: 'Firemen in working uniform, rubber coats, helmets, and boots. Thrilling rescue from burning building. Smoke effects are fine.' For projected films, the company produced *The Burning Stable* (1896), which 'shows a barn actually in flames, from which four horses and a burning wagon are rescued by firemen and stable hands. The scene is exciting, full of action from beginning to end.'[123]

This set in train a great number of films on the subject, from the street theatre of fire brigade demonstrations to staged fire scenes such as Warwick Trading Company's *Fire Call and Rescue by Fire Escapes* (1899). This joined two dramatised scenes together to make a 175-feet reel, with one showing a passer-by who, hearing cries and seeing smoke from an upper-storey window, runs to the fire station to give the alarm. The catalogue tells us that the firemen emerge and dash to the rescue. They carry a man and a woman down the ladders to safety. In the second film they attempt, semi-humorously, to put out the fire using various old-fashioned and newer bits of equipment.[124] Unfortunately this film doesn't survive, and we know nothing of who made it, but it seems to indicate a degree of narrative continuity,

R. W. Paul's *The Railway Collision* (1900).

while the man's progress between two different locations – the burning building and the fire station – must have involved an edit.

We know this scene well from James Williamson's *Fire!* (1901), which illustrates this astonishing advance. The scenario – firemen rescue people from a burning building – is the subject of many lantern shows, but in this film version a policemen runs from one shot and into another. As in the Warwick film, he discovers the building on fire in shot one, then runs out of the frame to the right. In shot two he runs in from the left to summon help from the fire station. This is true continuity editing as we understand it today. Williamson improves on the Warwick version by extending the story, rather than bolting on a demonstration of fire brigade technique. This provides the suspense: will the firemen arrive in time? In the following shots we see the burning building from the inside (the point of view of the trapped residents), then from the outside (the firemen rescuing people by ladder), in a basic 'shot/reverse shot' edit. This film seems to me the clearest candidate for the

James Williamson's *Fire!* (1901).

leap towards continuity editing that would make longer dramatic stories conceivable. When the film print was new and clear, we might even have seen some acting (the rescued man is played by Sam Dalton, Williamson's expressive lead actor, who featured in *The Big Swallow*). This might in turn have elicited some emotional or imaginative response from the audience – arguably the crucial element of narrative film's appeal.

By 1901 filmmakers had evolved techniques in which the narrative could be extended, not only by stringing together scenes in rough chronological order but with a seamless flow from one scene to the next. At the risk of falling into the trap of judging early films only for their contribution to the development of narrative cinema, we can see in these few surviving examples the germs of the fiction film which would one day dominate the story of cinema – or we can see in them a fascinating reflection of Victorian popular culture. Still, it's worth noting that the tableaux fiction film persisted into the 1900s, even as the film show began to establish itself in a home of its own.

Close-up: The Sound of Silents

The movies – at least British ones – sang before they could talk. *Kitty Mahone* (1900) stands as a unique surviving example of a British 'sound' film from the Victorian era. It features Lil Hawthorne, a well-known American music hall singer resident in London, and was made to be accompanied by a gramophone recording of her performing the song of the title (probably disc 3203, recorded by Berliner Gramophone).

It was made by Walter Gibbons, who had escaped from apprenticeship at a Wolverhampton nail factory by becoming first a touring singer, and then an energetic entrepreneur in the fledgling film business, with his own film show, the 'Gibbons Bio-tableaux', playing at the Hippodrome in London's West End. On the lookout for a competitive edge, Gibbons hatched the idea of bringing to the public films of their favourite music hall performers, with synchronised sound supplied by the gramophone companies. *Kitty Mahone* was made on an open-air stage, with a theatrical backdrop of a romantic gothic ruin borrowed for the occasion (you can see it gently billowing in the breeze), in front of which stood Hawthorne in male costume, singing the song of the title – one of her signature tunes. A further eight films (all lost) were made under the same 'Gibbons Phono-bio Tableaux' banner

Although relatively unsuccessful, Gibbons' venture illustrates filmmakers' ambitions, right from the start, to unite sound and picture. Sound recording, like moving pictures, had overcome all kinds of technical obstacles, but even so the marriage of the two would take longer than expected. Synchronisation had to wait for the photocell, triodes, motors that could be run in synch, suitable microphone and amplification technology and other developments that could be adapted for film.

It would have been very difficult to perform these films on a regular basis within the film show at a venue like the Hippodrome. No playback machine could yet muster enough amplification to fill more than a medium-sized room, while synchronisation was approximate at best and audio quality was poor. But at least people could imagine what it would be like to see and hear a film at the same time. Similar experiments were going on across the English

Kitty Mahone (1900).

Channel in 1900, and producers kept trying throughout the silent era, until the problem was finally solved in the late 1920s. In the meantime, filmmakers had to press on without it, finding live musical solutions that created a new, highly sophisticated – if ultimately doomed – art form: silent cinema.

Lil Hawthorne, meanwhile, would earn herself another mention in the annals of sound technology. She was instrumental in the capture of the notorious killer Dr Hawley Crippen, hanged in 1910 for the murder of his wife, Cora (herself an aspiring music hall singer, who went by the stage name Belle Elmore). Lil and her husband, John Nash, were friends of Cora's, and when she went missing, the couple helped to convince police that something was afoot. By the time Cora's body was found, Crippen and his lover were on a liner bound for Canada', but they were intercepted on board thanks to then-new wireless telegraphy. Hawthorne herself died in 1926, just too early to see in the age of the 'talkies'.

EPILOGUE: THE END OF ALL THINGS

Throughout this book I have focused largely on the surviving Victorian films as source material, extrapolating from them what the remainder might have been like. But how much more might we know if even a few of those 80% of lost films had survived? Are the films we have representative of what once existed? Broadly, I think they are. Having read the descriptions of early films in filmographies and the filmmakers' catalogues of the day, I think we have examples of every type, category or genre. But of course individual films bring their own unique attractions, and there are films I long to rediscover. Top of my list would be G. A. Smith's *Snapshotting an Audience*, mainly because of its intriguing premise, with its photographer trying to pose the restless audience 'before whom this picture is shown'.[125] Perhaps that habit that early filmmakers had of copying each other's work can help us. An American remake, *Photographing the Audience* (1901), by notorious film pirate Siegmund Lubin, evidently added its own twist:

> 'Finally [the photographer] snaps the camera in despair, but it explodes and wrecks the surroundings. He is so incensed that he hurls pieces of the stage furniture into the audience.'[126]

But did this new ending add drama to Smith's original, or comedy? And what were Smith's 'surroundings'? Was his audience, like Lubin's, in a theatre – perhaps a music hall, as in Paul's *The Countryman and the Cinematograph*, or an open-air auditorium like Smith's Pleasure Gardens in Hove? I'd like to see the audience, even a fictional one, and the camera turned back on its viewers; the film seems to have been, like Williamson's *The Big Swallow*, an example of film's emerging consciousness of itself.

For similar reasons, I'd love to see a pair of Smith's films that relate aesthetically to the art of filmmaking. *The Haunted Picture Gallery* featured rows of portraits, simulating a strip of film frames, out of which living characters step. *Making Sausages; or the End of All Things* (1897) was Smith's take on a hoary old pantomime gag, first filmed by the Lumière brothers, in which a grinding machine is fed live cats, dogs and old boots, which emerge as a neat string of sausages. A version of this film (although I'm not completely convinced it is Smith's) did turn up recently, which gives us hope that others may yet be rediscovered.[127] It's a neat metaphor for the early film production process: feeding not cats or dogs, but waves, trains or crowds into its own hand-cranked machine – the camera – and turning them into a string of little films.

Some lost films captured moments of history. It would be intriguing to see *Dance of Abyssinian Priests before the Ark of the Covenant* (1901), filmed for the Warwick Trading Company, even if it probably shows only the outside of the church in which the Ark is said to be contained. Had Biograph's *Demonstration in Front of the Palace Theatre* survived, we would at least have *one* of the two missing films of the extraordinary 'Mafeking night' of 18 May 1900, when Londoners took to the streets in carnivalesque celebration of Baden-Powell's morale-boosting victory in the Boer War. Others deprive us of rare moments of screen history. *Panorama Taken in a Steam Crane* (1900), photographed by Arthur Cooper for Birt Acres, was a kind of dizzying vertical panorama, for which the cameraman, seated in a bucket, was dropped 100 feet while filming. And talking of Acres, I'd like to see film of the man himself in *Panorama – Highgate Tunnel – Goods train* (1895), which, according to Denis Gifford, showed 'a GNR luggage train passing a man (Birt Acres) on platform'.[128]

The first mountaineering film, advertised in Warwick's catalogue of 1897–98, sounds unusually thrilling: following a party of climbers on an ascent of Mont Blanc, during which one of them falls into a crevasse and has to be rescued. Film's obsession with the exploration of the natural world starts here. Of the very rare natural history films of this period, Warwick Trading Company's *The Octopus* (1901) – featuring, the catalogue tells us, a 'captive "devil-fish" writhing'[129] – was probably the first film of this subject ever made, preceding Charles Urban's 1903 study (also lost) and nearly three decades before Jean Painlevé's celebrated film of 1928.

The very title of *Negro Women Coaling a Vessel* (1901) is offensive today, but had this film from Warwick's Jamaica and British West Indies series survived, it might have offered an important corrective to early films' near-total negation of the uglier side of Empire. All those steamers and navy ships we see in Victorian films had to be refuelled at strategically-placed, well-defended depots around the world. The backbreaking work of heaving the coal into the ship's hold was frequently left to colonial labourers, in this case women, one basket at a time. The subject of numerous paintings, photographs and illustrations, it was a visually striking but thoroughly objectifying display of imperial exploitation. Western notions of the 'exotic' were often played on by street performers of magic. I wish we could see Warwick's *Hindoo Snake Charmer Performing the Mango* (1901) – not for its 'exoticism' but for its recording of what was, like the legendary rope trick, a favourite piece of street magic: the magician plants a mango seed, covers it with a basket and waters it, then uncovers it to reveal a fully grown mango plant. Even an inkling of how that looked would be fascinating.

Given the fragility of the medium, we should be grateful that any have survived at all, but it can be frustrating when we have only fragments of films. How much more illustrative of the Victorian film show would the extra scenes of Paul's *The Countryman and the Cinematograph* (1901) be? What more might his *The Magic Sword* (1901) tell us about pantomime stagecraft?

But we can, today, see the surviving films with extraordinary ease. In 2018, the BFI National Archive's completed its project to digitise all its films from this era and make them available online, free, across the UK. Seeing these short films online accentuates their kinship with today's online moving image media. We might watch Tom Green gurning for the camera in one click and, in the next, a YouTube film of a child pulling silly faces. Or see Lil Hawthorne lip-synching to Kitty Mahone in 1900 alongside a TikTok video of a girl miming to her favourite song in 2021.

Our understanding of the very early days of film has undergone a radical change in the last 20 years, and not only because of this new accessibility. The BFI's digitisation project went back to the original celluloid films, rather than reproduce poor quality duplicates made decades ago. The resulting boost in image quality helps us appreciate how the films must have looked when new. Large-format films (60mm or 68mm) from companies such as British Biograph, Gaumont and Prestwich, can be of particularly astounding quality – so much so that audiences sometimes struggle to accept their authenticity. We're lucky too, to have recovered films lost for generations. The Mitchell and Kenyon cache found in 1994 transformed our understanding of the filmmaking environment in the late-Victorian era.

A great deal of excellent research work has been done in recent years, often showcased at specialist silent film festivals such as the Giornate del Cinema Muto in Pordenone or the Cinema Ritrovato in Bologna, while in the UK, the British Silent Film Festival has for more than two decades been on a mission to screen and study all of the nation's surviving silent films. A host of resourceful and knowledgeable researchers and writers have built on the work of pioneers like John Barnes, Rachael Low, Barry Salt and Denis Gifford, producing biographies of the era's greatest filmmakers and studies of industry, subject and genre. Thanks to them, we are correcting inaccuracies in earlier histories and leaving behind unhelpful assumptions about early film's 'primitivism', and distracting debates about who 'invented cinema', and gaining a better understanding of the specificities of the era.

I think it is demonstrable that, for all the continuities, there is something significantly and perceptibly different between the films of the Victorian years and those that followed. The years from 1896 to 1901 witnessed extraordinary developments in the medium: longer films, multi-part and multi-scene films, an expanding lexicon of shots and the establishment and rapid evolution of film language, not to mention diversification and specialisation in film genres, and the emergence of new forms of programming, marketing and showmanship. For me, the most striking feature of the era, which comes across strongly in the films and the contemporary accounts, is the tangible excitement of the filmmakers, the developers of the technology, the exhibitors and the audiences. People of the time were not only captivated by the novelty of film; they seem to have instinctively understood that the coming of moving pictures marked a profound shift in the way they saw the world and how the future world would see *them*. History was no longer the sole preserve of the written word.

It's striking, too, just how commercially driven early filmmaking was. Initial success impelled filmmakers to experiment with what the camera could do, to adapt existing entertainments to the new form and, above all, to copy anything that seemed to resonate with audiences. This tactic led to waves of fads and fashions in the developing industry, from local films to facials, and from phantom rides to Boer War 'reconstructions'. We can now easily trace these through contemporary advertisements in the trade and regular press. The abundance of easily accessible material allows us to scrutinise these changes as they were going on across the country in a given moment. We can see genres and subgenres come and go, but none of these very specifically Victorian genres disappeared absolutely. Instead they were, over time, subsumed into other genres or into the language of film itself: facials become close-ups or emblematic shots at the ends of comedies; phantom rides evolve into travelling shots; local films are absorbed into newsreels and cinemagazines.

In these first few years a great many of the possibilities of the new medium were explored, which makes it a very fertile period of film to study if we're interested in anything from aesthetic and technological developments to the commercial contexts and physical and social environments in which films were viewed. One advantage of breaking out of the traditional linear history of the cinema and concentrating on the films themselves is that we are free to see parallels between their content and their audience appeal and those of other forms that preceded or postdated them – whether 19th century theatre and music hall, Edwardian newsreels, mid-20th century television or the moving image products of today's online platforms.

Equally, people interested in different aspects and periods of moving image history may be struck by what they discover in the era of Victorian film: those researching the growth of 'cinema' can uncover very early signs of narrative development, while those studying documentary or moving image journalism will find much to study in in actuality and topicals. Anyone fascinated by 'user-generated' online moving image, meanwhile, may notice surprising resonances with Victorian trick films, facials, panoramas or phantom rides.

If we look to film as a historical source, what can these films tell us about the Victorians of the 1890s? The term 'Victorian' perhaps carries too much baggage; as Lytton Strachey quipped, 'The history of the Victorian age will never be written: we know too much about it.'[130] We might say the same of Elizabeth II's reign. But what can we trace of those qualities we associate with the Victorian age: evangelism, imperialism, industrialism, rigid class and gender divides, an obsession with respectability? The passion for pageantry is manifest, and with it all the trappings of Empire; the prejudices of the times are present in all sorts of glaring or incidental ways. And yet the people in these films feel surprisingly modern and familiar. Certainly, these late Victorians don't seem much like Dickens' Victorians, any more than the lives of the readers of this book resemble the lives of those of the 1950s, at the beginning of Elizabeth II's reign.

It's the privilege of generations alive today to be able to see more of the past in moving images than any before them, and in better quality, too. Through the surviving films we can immerse ourselves in the world of the late Victorians – it is inspiring to spend time in their company.

TABLES

TABLE 1: BRITISH FILM CATALOGUE*

	Total films (Gifford)†	Fiction films	% of total	Non-fiction films	% of total	Military subjects (non-fiction)	% of non-fiction
1895	29	4	14%	25	86%	–	–
1896	144	31	22%	113	78%	14	10%
1897	311	42	14%	269	86%	101	32%
1898	602	101	17%	501	83%	85	14%
1899	744	118	16%	626	84%	193	26%
1900	831	122	15%	709	85%	388	47%
1901	734	130	18%	604	82%	123	17%
Total	3,395	548	16%	2,847	84%	904	27%

TABLE 2: MITCHELL AND KENYON FILMS ABSENT FROM BRITISH FILM CATALOGUE ‡

	Total films	Fiction films	% of total	Non-fiction films*	% of total	Military subjects (non-fiction)	% of non-fiction
1899	3	3	100%	–	–	–	–
1900	102	13	13%	89	87%	13	15%
1901	165	17	10%	148	90%	28	19%
Total	270	33	12%	237	88%	41	17%

* Figures are derived from Denis Gifford's two-volume British Film Catalogue, which was compiled from early filmmakers' catalogues and from the photographic and stage trade press.

Documentation of early film is patchy. Many manufacturers' catalogues are lost, while film titles weren't always fixed and surviving copies rarely have printed titles attached. Some films didn't make it into a catalogue at all (see Table 2), so weren't picked up by Gifford's research.

I have included the films made by Birt Acres for the kinetoscope, as they were used for projection. But I have omitted pre-1895 'films' never exhibited for the public, such as those of Louis le Prince, William Friese Greene and Wordsworth Donisthorpe.

† Where films were issued as multi-part series, each part is counted as one film.

‡ Figures reflect Mitchell and Kenyon titles rediscovered by Peter Worden in 1995, which were are not in the British Film Catalogue. Some dates are estimates, based on the the best data available.

Since Mitchell and Kenyon produced no catalogues, we have no way of knowing how many more of the titles they produced remain lost.

RECOMMENDED READING

FILM HISTORY

John Barnes, *The Beginnings of the Cinema in England 1894 to 1901*, Vols 1–5 (London: Bishopsgate Press, 1983; digital edition: Exeter University Press, 2015)

Rachael Low & Roger Manvell, *The History of the British Film 1896–1906* (London: George Allen & Unwin Ltd, 1973)

Denis Gifford, *A Catalogue of British Film, Vol 1: Fiction* (London: Routledge, 2000)

Denis Gifford, *A Catalogue of British Film Vol 2: Non-Fiction* (London: Routledge, 2001)

Richard Brown & Barry Anthony, *A Victorian Film Enterprise: the History of the British Mutoscope and Biograph Company, 1897–1915*, (Wiltshire: Flicks Books, 1999)

Simon Popple & Colin Harding, *In the Kingdom of Shadows: A Companion to Early Cinema* (London: Cygnus Arts, 1996)

Simon Popple & Joe Kember, *Early Cinema: From Factory Gate to Film Factory* (London: Wallflower Press, 2004)

Richard Abel (ed), *Encyclopedia of Early Cinema* (London, New York: Routledge, 2011)

Harold Brown, *Physical Characteristics of Early Films as Aids to Identification* New Expanded Edition. Camille Blot Wellens (Brussels: FIAF, 2020)

Barry Salt, *Film Style and Technology: History and Analysis* (London: Starword, 2003)

Tony Fletcher, *Regulating the Cinematograph in London 1897- 1906* (London: Local History Publications, 2017)

Tony Fletcher, *The Kinematograph Theatre Arrives: Part III of The London County Council and the Cinematograph* (London: Local History Publications, 2021)

ONLINE RESOURCES

BFI Player's Victorian Film collection includes all the surviving Victorian films, free within the UK https://player.bfi.org.uk/free/collection/victorian-film

Stephen Herbert & Luke Mckernan's *Who's Who of Victorian Cinema* (London: BFI, 1996) is online at https://www.victorian-cinema.net/

The Bioscope, Luke McKernan's archived blog on early film: https://thebioscope.net/

Adam Matthews Digital's Victorians on Film resource reproduces the BFI player collection for international scholars:
https://www.victoriansonfilm.amdigital.co.uk/

BIOGRAPHIES OF FILMMAKERS

Paul Spehr, *WKL Dickson: The Man Who Made the Movies* (Eastleigh: John Libbey & Co, 2008)

Ian Christie, *Robert Paul and the Origins of British Cinema* (Chicago, University of Chicago Press, 2019)

Frank Gray, *The Brighton School and the Birth of British Film* (London: Palgrave Macmillan, 2019)

Luke McKernan, *A Yank in Britain: The Lost Memoirs of Charles Urban, Film Pioneer* (Exeter: Exeter University Press, 1999)

Martin Sopocy, *James Williamson: Studies and Documents of a Pioneer of the Film Narrative* (Cranbury, Fairleigh Dickinson University Press, 1998)

VICTORIAN HISTORY

David Gange, *The Victorians* (London: Oneworld Publications Beginner's Guides, 2016)

David Newsome, *The Victorian World Picture: Perceptions and Introspections in an Age of Change* (London: John Murray, 1997)

CONTEMPORARY SOURCES

British Journal of Photography

The British Newspaper Archive carries a huge range of contemporary newspapers, magazines and journals. The most useful for early film, music hall, theatre and fairground trades are *The Era*, *The Stage*, *The World's Fair*, and *The Showman*. Also the illustrated press, e.g. *The Illustrated London News*, *The Sketch*, *The Graphic* are useful for film related stories. *The Bioscope* and *The Kinematograph Weekly* are later trade papers for the film industry and contain occasional memoirs of pioneer filmmakers for the Victorian years.

NOTES

1. John B. Kuiper paper read at the Society of American Archivists, Oct. 19, 1967 (references to Barbara Deming and Penelope Houston come from this paper).
2. J. Miller Barr, 'Animated Pictures', in *Popular Science Monthly*, December 1897, p. 178.
3. Ibid., p. 179.
4. John Fell, 'Pioneers of the British Film: review', *Film Quarterly*, Summer 1989, p. 47.
5. Richard Maltby, introduction to John Barnes, *The Beginnings of Cinema in England, Vol. 5: 1900*, (Exeter: University of Exeter Press, 1997), pp. xi–xxxii.
6. Ian Christie, *Robert Paul and the Origins of British Cinema* (Chicago: Chicago University Press, 2019).
7. Frank Gray's *The Brighton School and the Birth of British Film* (London: Palgrave Macmillan, 2019) is an in-depth examination of the film careers of G. A. Smith and James Williamson.
8. Tom Gunning, 'The Cinema of Attraction(s): Early Film, Its Spectator and the Avant-Garde' in Thomas Elsaessar, *Early Cinema: Space, Frame, Narrative* (London: BFI, 1985).
9. Barbara Deming, 'The Library of Congress Film project: Exposition of a method' *The Library of Congress Quarterly Journal of Current Acquisitions*, vol. 2, no. 1, November 1944, pp. 3–36.
10. Penelope Houston, 'The Nature of the Evidence' in *Sight and Sound*, 36, pp. 88–92 (Spring 1967).
11. The index of A. N. Wilson's *The Victorians* (London: Arrow Books, 2002), judged by fellow historian Adam Roberts 'the best single-volume work on the Victorian age yet written', includes not a single reference to films or filmmakers.
12. Deming, 'The Library of Congress Film project', p. 14.
13. *The Era*, cited in Barnes, *The Beginnings of the Cinema in England, Vol 1* (Exeter: Exeter University Press, 1976), p. 19.

14. The manager of the music hall in Marcel Carné's *Les Enfants du Paradis* (France, 1945).
15. Robert Paul, 'Before 1910: Kinematograph Experiences' in *Proceedings of the British Kinematograph Society no. 38* (London: BKS, 1936).
16. The term 'primitive' has frequently been applied to early film, most notably by Noël Burch, in his concept of the 'Primitive Mode of Representation' as contrasted with the dominant 'Institutional Mode of Representation' (Burch, *Une Praxis du cinema*, 1969). 'Primitive' was not intended pejoratively, but to signify a film language untainted by bourgeois associations, in a way analogous to 'primitivism' in fine art. But to those unfamiliar with art theory it is often read as simply 'crude'. The BFI itself used this term in its VHS/ DVD compilation 'Early Cinema: Primitives and Pioneers' in 2001. For the avoidance of confusion it is best abandoned altogether. For an in-depth examination see Bloom, PJ (2009). 'Refiguring the Primitive: Institutional Legacies of the Filmology Movement'. *Cinémas*, vol. 19, nos. 2–3, pp. 169–82.
17. 'The Alhambra' (review) in *The Era*, 23 February 1895, p. 16.
18. *Harmsworth Magazine*, Feb–Jul 1901, reprinted in Charlie Holland, *Strange, Feats and Clever Turns: Remarkable Speciality Acts at the Turn of the 20th Century as Seen by Their Contemporaries* (London: Holland & Palmer, 1998).
19. The offensive term 'Kaffir' was widely used in the colonial era as a collective term for Black Southern Africans. George Chirgwin adopted the black face from the minstrel acts of his youth, adding an idiosyncratic white diamond around one eye.
20. Michael Chanan (1996), *The Dream That Kicks: The Prehistory and Early Years of Cinema in Britain* (London: Routledge), p. 24.
21. Birt Acres, letter in the *Daily Chronicle*, 23 June 1898, p. 4.
22. Robert Paul, letter in the *Daily Chronicle*, 25 June 1898, p. 8.
23. Anonymous letter in the *Daily Chronicle*, 24 June 1898, p. 4.
24. Barnes, *The Beginnings of Cinema in England, Vol. 2* (Exeter: Exeter University Press, 1996); Luke McKernan, https://thebioscope.net/?s=jubilee&submit=Search (accessed 12 December 2022).
25. *The Era*, 24 July 1897, p 16, quoted in Barnes, Ibid., p. 2.
26. Stephen Bottomore (2007), *Filming, Faking and Propaganda: The Origins of the War Film, 1897–1902* (unpublished PhD thesis).
27. *The Photogram*, July 1900.
28. Obituary for Charles Morton, *The Era*, October 1904.
29. *Strand Magazine*, 1896 XII (Jul to Dec), p. 140.

30. *The Photogram*, July 1899, p. 224, quoted in Barnes, *The Beginnings of the Cinema in England, Vol. 4* (Exeter: Exeter University Press, 1996), p. 124.
31. Cecil Hepworth, quoted in Barnes, *The Beginnings of the Cinema in England, Vol. 2*, p. 158.
32. *The Photogram*, vol. 4, no. 39 (March 1897), p. 78, quoted in Barnes, *The Beginnings of Cinema in England, Vol. 2*.
33. Based on Denis Gifford's *British Film Catalogue Vol. II, Non-Fiction* (London: Routledge, 2001) and the BFI National Archive data on Mitchell and Kenyon collection.
34. Richard Maltby, in Barnes, *The Beginnings of Cinema in England, Vol. 5* (Exeter: University of Exeter Press, 1997), p. 32.
35. *The Era*, 19 August, 1899, p. 24b, quoted in Barnes, *The Beginnings of the Cinema in England, Vol. 4*, p. 23.
36. Stephen Bottomore, *Filming, Faking and Propaganda: the Origins of War Films 1897–1902*, unpublished PhD thesis University of Utrecht, footnote 88.
37. Alfred J. West, *Sea Salts and Celluloid*, (unpublished, 1936), p. 17.
38. *Amateur Photographer*, cited in Barnes, *The Beginnings of Cinema in England, Vol. 3* (Exeter: University of Exeter Press, 1997).
39. R. W. Paul catalogue, 1901/2.
40. Hilaire Belloc, *The Modern Traveller* (1898).
41. Northcliffe papers, 26 March 1900, quoted in Paul Jonathan Meller, *The Development of Modern Propaganda in Britain 1854–1902*, Durham University doctoral thesis (2010), p. 197.
42. Jonathan Rose, *The Intellectual Life of the British Working Classes* (Yale, 2002) pp. 335–7, quoted in Meller, *The Development of Modern Propaganda in Britain*, p. 197.
43. William Kennedy Laurie Dickson, *The Biograph in Battle: Its Story in the South African War* (London: T. Fisher Unwin, 1901).
44. Ibid., p. 109.
45. *The Era*, 20 November, 1897, p. 21.
46. Filmed respectively as *Bloemfontein: Unfurling the Flag* and *Lord Roberts Hoisting the Union Jack at Pretoria* (both 1900).
47. Obituary for Charles Morton, *The Morning Post*, 19 October 1904, p. 4.
48. See, for example, Barry Salt, *Film Style and Technology: History and Analysis* (2nd edition, London: Starwood, 1992).

49. The Mitchell and Kenyon collection was discovered in 1994 by local Blackburn historian Peter Worden, and the bulk of it (minus some 100 films, largely fiction, most of which were acquired by London's Cinema Museum) was acquired by the BFI National Archive in 2000 and released to the general public in 2004–05.
50. *The Lost World of Mitchell & Kenyon* (BBC, 2005).
51. A few of the films were taken in Scotland, Wales and Ireland, but Mitchell and Kenyon seem rarely to have ventured south of the Midlands.
52. Tom Gunning, 'Pictures of Crowd Splendour: the Mitchell and Kenyon Factory Gate Films', in Vanessa Toulmin, Simon Popple & Patrick Russell (Eds.) (2004), *The Lost World of Mitchell and Kenyon: Edwardian Britain of Film* (London: BFI), p, 55.
53. See Vanessa Toulmin (2006), *Electric Edwardians: The Story of the Mitchell & Kenyon Collection* (London: BFI/Palgrave), and the DVD collection *Electric Edwardians: The films of Mitchell and Kenyon* (BFI, 2005).
54. *The Hull Times*, 13 October 1910, cited in Vanessa Toulmin (2001), 'Local Films for Local People' in *Film History*, vol. 13, no. 2, p. 137.
55. *The Showman*, 9 August 1901, cited in Toulmin, 'Local Films for Local People', p. 131.
56. Cecil Hepworth (1951), *Came the Dawn: Memories of a Film Pioneer* (London: Phoenix House), pp. 58–9.
57. Bankruptcy notice in *The Times*, 26 November 1902., p. 3
58. David A. Cook, *A History of Narrative Cinema*, fifth edition, p. 15.
59. Paul Dave, 'Knocking Off Time in the North: Images of the Working Class and History in L. S. Lowry and Mitchell and Kenyon', in *Heading North: The North of England in Film and Television*, Mazierska, Ewa (Ed.) (London: Palgrave, 2017), p. 53.
60. Dave analyses the crowd movements of the factory gate films in terms of criteria in Elias Canetti's classic study *Crowds and Power* (1960).
61. Plunkett, J., 2013. 'Moving Panoramas *c.* 1800 to 1840: The Spaces of Nineteenth-Century Picture-Going' in *19: Interdisciplinary Studies in the Long Nineteenth Century*, no. 17.
62. One review of a (lost) phantom ride noted, 'The apparent movement of the rapidly-passing landscape is so realistic that it creates quite a peculiar feeling in the onlooker, and the picture is loudly applauded.' (*The Era*, 10 September 1898, p. 18).
63. *Evening Standard*, 16 November 1897, p. 6.
64. Rachael Low and Roger Manvell, *The History of the British Film 1896–1906* (London: Allen & Unwin, 1973), p. 71.
65. Hepworth catalogue, 1903, p. 19.

66. Ibid., p. 22.
67. Ibid., p. 13.
68. Low and Manvell, *The History of the British Film 1896–1906*, p. 74.
69. *The London Gazette*, 19 May 1899, p. 3186.
70. Quoted in Deac Rossell (2017) 'Rough Sea at Dover: a Genealogy', in *Early Popular Visual Culture*, vol. 15, no. 1, pp. 59–82.
71. *Amateur Photographer*, vol. 23, 24 January 1896, p. 75.
72. Catalogue for the 2016 Cinema Ritrovato Film Festival, p. 34.
73. Miriam Hansen, *Babel and Babylon: Spectatorship in American Silent Film* (Cambridge, Mass.: Harvard University Press, 1994), p. 29.
74. Lynda Neade, *The Haunted Gallery: Painting, Photography, Film around 1900* (Newhaven, Conn.: Yale University Press, 2007), pp. 103–4.
75. *British Journal of Photography*, 23 April 1897, quoted in Barnes, *The Beginnings of the Cinema in England, Vol. 2*, p. 199.
76. *The Era*, 18 August 1900, p. 14.
77. The Filoscope was a flicker-book device patented by Henry Short, a cameraman for Robert Paul.
78. *Brighton Gazette*, 31 December 1896, p. 8.
79. *The Sketch*, 20 September 1899, p. 1.
80. *The Tatler*, 2 October 1901, p. 22.
81. Williamson catalogue, 1902.
82. The famous clown Joseph Grimaldi is first recorded using it in 'Harlequin and Poor Robin' in 1823: see David Mayer, *Harlequin in his Element, The English Pantomime, 1806–1836*, (Cambridge, Mass.: Harvard University Press, 1969), p. 217.
83. Frederick A. Talbot, *Moving Pictures: How They Are Made and Worked* (London: J. B. Lippincott, 1912).
84. Warwick catalogue, 1897–8, p. 5.
85. R. W. Paul catalogue, 1901.
86. Robert Paul used titles or, as he describes them, 'letter press' cards, in *General Servant Difficulties* (1900) and *Scrooge* (1901).
87. The phrase 'Oh, Mother Will be Pleased!' has baffled generations of historians – it may have been the refrain to a popular song still in the popular memory from 1879, performed by Herbert Campbell. See also Barry Anthony, *The King's Jester: The Life of Dan Leno, Victorian Comic Genius* (London: I. B. Tauris, 2010), p. 76.
88. Listed in Barnes, *The Beginnings of Cinema in England, Vol 5*, p. 6.

89. *The Stage*, 29 January 1886, p. 13.

90. George's Sadoul – George Méliès (Paris, Seghers: 1961) quoted by Tom Gunning (1990), 'The Cinema of Attractions: Early Film, Its Spectator and the Avant-Garde', in *Early Cinema: Space, Frame, Narative*, Thomas Elsaesser and Adam Barker (Eds.) (London: BFI), p. 57.

91. Hepworth catalogue, 1903, p. 43.

92. Williamson's Kinematograph Films catalogue, 1899.

93. For the history of the Harlequinade in early Victorian England see David Mayer, *Harlequin in his Element: the English Pantomime 1806–1836* (Harvard, 1969); Bryony Dixon, *Chaplin and the Harlequinade* (http://chaplin.bfi.org.uk/programme/essays/harlequinade.html: accessed 18/10/2021); Jeffrey Richards, *Harlequinade and the Golden Age of Pantomime* (https://theibtaurisblog.com/2014/12/19/harlequinade-and-the-golden-age-of-pantomime: accessed 18/10/2021).

94. Advertisement in *The Era*, 24 December 1898.

95. The film is also sometimes to Max Skladaowsky of Germany: see Harold Brown, *Physical Characteristics of Early Films as Aids to Identification* (expanded edition, Ed. Camille Blot-Wellens, Bruxelles: FIAF, 2020).

96. See Pathé catalogues on database of Fondation Jerôme Seydoux http://filmographie.fondation-jeromeseydoux-pathe.com.

97. Barnes, *The Beginnings of the Cinema in England, Vol. 5*, p. 72.

98. Elias Koopman, *Daily Telegraph*, 31 December 1898, p. 5.

99. See Tables, p. 176.

100. Richard Brown and Barry Anthony, *A Victorian Enterprise: the History of the British Mutoscope and Biograph Company 1897–1915*, (Trowbridge: Flicks Books, 1999), p 215.

101. See Tables, p. 176.

102. J. Miller Barr, in *Popular Science Monthly*, vol. 52, December 1897, p. 194.

103. The sketch was a short dramatic form, performed in music halls, without dialogue and limited by law to 18 minutes. This was so as not to compete with the longer plays with dialogue that were the preserve of the legitimate theatres. In 1899 the permitted running time of a sketch was extended to 30 minutes.

104. The film starred veteran actor Jefferson in his signature role, and was photographed by Billy Bitzer, who would later work with DW Griffith.

105. '"King John" at Her Majesty's', *The Sketch*, 27 September 1899, p. 413.

106. Yet to be identified paper in the Graeme Cruickshank Theatre Collection, cited by Brown and Anthony, *A Victorian Enterprise*, p. 241, n. 48.

107. *Photographic News*, 8 April 1898, cited in Simon Popple and Colin Harding, *In the Kingdom of Shadows: A Companion to Early Cinema* (London: Cygnus Arts, 1996), p. 89.
108. *Financial Times*, 6 June 1899, cited in Brown and Anthony, *A Victorian Enterprise*, p. 65.
109. Barnes, *The Beginnings of the Cinema in England, Vol. 3*, p. 15.
110. Advertisement in *The Era*, cited in cited in Barnes, Ibid.
111. There were at least three Faust films circulating in 1898: Méliès *Faust et Marguerite*, Lumière's *Faust: apparition de Méphistophélès* and the Smith film. Phillip Woolf's press advertisements in *The Era* that year seem to suggest Smith's film was called *Faust and Gretchen*. It also appears as *Faust and Mephistopheles*.
112. B. Hasenfratz, 'Rethinking Early Cinematic Adaptations: Death of Poor Joe (1901)', *Nineteenth Century Theatre and Film*, vol. 42, no. 2 (2015), pp. 124–45.
113. *The Era,* 30 November 1900, p. 32.
114. Gunning, 'The Cinema of Attractions: Early Film, Its Spectator and the Avant-Garde', p. 65.
115. Warwick Trading Co. advertisement, *The Era*, 4 January 1902, p. 30.
116. Gunning, 'The Cinema of Attractions'.
117. Low and Manvell, *The History of the British Film 1896–1906*.
118. Robert Paul, *Proceedings of the British Kinematograph Society*, no. 38 (3 February 1936), p. 5.
119. A. C. Bromhead, lecture to British Kinematographic Society, 3 February 1936, quoted in Low and Manvell, *The History of the British Film 1896–1906*, p. 69.
120. C. K. Shorter, in *British Journal of Photography*, 28 April 1899, quoted in Stephen Bottomore, *Filming, Faking and Propaganda: The Origins of the War Film 1897–1902*, p. 39.
121. *Pall Mall Gazette*, 31 January 1900, quoted in Bottomore, *Filming, Faking and Propaganda*, p. 44.
122. *Church Times*, 3 August 1900, quoted in Bottomore, *Filming, Faking and Propaganda* p. 128.
123. Maguire & Baucus: Edison Films, supp. catalogue, January 20 1897, p. 2.
124. Warwick Trading Co. catalogue, 1901, p. 91.
125. Ibid., p. 167.
126. Lubin catalogue, 1907, p. 22.
127. It seems as if nearly every early film company filmed its own version of this gag – three were made by the American Biograph Co. alone (https://www.youtube.com/watch?v=lfo7v2rWY5c: accessed 1/10/2021).

128. Denis Gifford, *The British Film Catalogue, Vol. 2: Non-Fiction Film 1888–1994* (London: Routledge, 2001).
129. Warwick Trading Company catalogue, 1902, p. 38.
130. Lytton Stachey, Preface to *Eminent Victorians* (London: Chatto & Windus. 1918).

INDEX

Index entries in **bold** indicate illustrations.

20,000 Employees Entering Lord Armstrong's Elswick Works (1900) **85**
Acres, Birt 18, **19**, 22, 31, 37, **53**, 55, 56, 67, 101, 114, 115, 160, 163, 171
Admiral Cigarettes (1897) 124
Agoust Family of Jugglers (1898) **30**
Alice in Wonderland (1903) 163
American Biograph at the Palace (1899) **22**, 27
American Mutoscope and Biograph Company 27, 98, 158
Appleton, Richard James 41
Are You There? (1901) 149, 150, **150**
Army Life (1900) 70, 90, 156
Arrest of a Bookmaker (1898) 163
Arrest of a Deserter (1898) 159
Arrest of a Pickpocket (1895) 160, 163
Arrival of Train-load of Visitors at Henley Station (1899) **56**, 59
Arroseur Arrosé, L' (1895) 56
Artistic Creation (1901) 152, **152**
As Seen by a Telescope (1900) 148, **148**
Attack on a China Mission (1900) 73
Attack on a Mission Station (1900) 45
Aunt Selina (1900) **153**
Bamforth Company 146, 147
Barbe bleu (1901) 160, 162
Barber Saw the Joke, The (c.1900) 142, **142**
Barnes, John 11, 12, 16, 40, 159, 160, 173
Bathers, The (1900) **63**, 136
Battle of Spion Kop (1900) 75–6, **76**, 119
Battle of the Somme, The (1916) 41, 79
Battleship Odin Firing all Her Guns (1900) 67
Bayley, Eva 130, 140
Bayley, Laura 18, **19**, 30, 122, 146, 147, 150, 161
Beautiful Panorama of Railway from St. Germans Mill Bay (1900) **108**
Beheading a Chinese Boxer (1900) 46, **46**
Beheading of a Chinese Boxer (1900) 73
Big Swallow, The (1901) 151, **153**, 167, 171
Blackfriars Bridge (1896) 59
Bombardment of Mafeking (1899) 163
Booth, Walter 126, 128, 152
Bride's First Night, The (1898) 147

British Mutoscope and Biograph Company 24, 27, 39, 47, 48, 59, 62, 67, 71, 77, 78, 98, 99, 100, 106, 112, 119, 120, 125, 131, 140, 145, 154, 157, 158, 159, 171, 173
Burning Stable, The (1896) 165

Campbell, Herbert 28, 31, 131, 141, 180
Chamberlain, Joseph 38
Charge of the 12th Lancers (1899) **65**, 67
Cheese Mites; Or, Lilliputians in a London Restaurant (1901) 135, **135**
Cheetham, Arthur 117
Children Dancing to a Barrel Organ (1898) 55, 56
Children in the Nursery (1898) **63**
Children Playing on the Beach at Rhyl (1898) 117
Chinese Magic Extraordinary (1901) 135
Churchill, Winston 43
Churned Waters (1898) 117
Cinderella (1898) 133, 160, 161
Cinderella (1899) 160
Cinematographic View of the Royal Albert Bridge, A (1901) 100
Clown and Police (1900) 144, **145**
Clown Barber (1898) 132
Collings, Esmé 117, 148
Come Along Do! (1898) 149
Comic Costume Race (1896) 31
Comic Grimacer (1900) 141
Co-operative Wholesale Clothing Factory in Manchester 86
Corsican Brothers, The (1898) 133, 161
Countryman and the Cinematograph, The (1901) **26**, 27, 150, 170, 172
Cricketer Jumping over Garden Gate (1895) 31
Crowds outside St George's Hall in Bradford (1901) 88

D. Devant Prestidigitation (1897) 129
Dalton, Sam 150, 167
Dance of Abyssinian Priests before the Ark of the Covenant (1901) 171
Danseuses des rues (1896) 55
Daring Daylight Robbery, A (1903) 163
Darwen Factory Gate (1901) 48
Death of Poor Joe, The (1900) 30, 161, **161**

Demonstration in Front of the Palace Theatre (1900) 171
Deonzo Brothers, The (1901) **28**, 29
Départ de Jerusalem en chemin de fer (1897) 98
Derby, The (1895) 53, **53**
Devant, David 30, 128, 129
Dickson, William Kennedy Laurie 18, **19**, 23, 24, 28, 39, 43, 44, 45, 50, 62, 67, 74, 75, 77, 99, 158, 159, 162
Difficulties of an Animated Photographer (1898) 30
Dispatch Bearer (1900) 164, **164**
Diving for Treasure (1900) 136
Dog Outwits the Kidnappers, The (1908) 138
Dr Macintyre's X-Ray Film (1896) 121, **122**
Drill of the Kansas City Fire Department (1899) 61, **61**
Duel to the Death (1898) 157
Dull Razor, A (1900) 140

Eccentric Dancer, The (1900) 138
Edison Company 23, 124, 165
Edison, Thomas 38, 56, 159
Edward VII, King 11, 43
Egg Laying Man, The (1896) 129
Empire State Express (1896) 99
Employees Leaving Alexandra Docks, Liverpool (1901) 100
Employees Leaving Brown's Atlas Works, Sheffield (1901) 48
Enfants pêchent des crevettes (1896) 117
Entrée du cinematographe (1896) **25**, 26, 86
Explosion of a Motor Car (1900) 138, **138**, 145

Fateful Letter, The (1898) 140
Faust and Mephistopheles (1898) 134, 161
Faust et Marguerite (1898) 181
Faust: apparition de Méphistophélès (1898) 181
Fencing Contest from the Three Musketeers (1898) 157
Fire Call and Rescue by Fire Escapes (1899) 165
Fire Rescue Scene (1894) 165
Fire! (1901) 61, 166–7, **167**
Footpads (c.1897) 111, **111**, 163
Four Warships in Rough Seas 39, **66**, 67, **109**
Fun on the Clothes-Line (1896) **27**, 28
Funeral of Queen Victoria, Marble Arch (Hepworth, 1901) **42**
Funeral of Queen Victoria, Procession Starting from Victoria Station (1901) 43

Game of Snowballing, A (1898) **57**
Gaumont 62, 164, 173
General Buller Embarking on the Dunottar Castle (1899) 43
General Servant Difficulties (1900) 180
Gibbons Bio-Tableaux 81
Gibbons, Walter 28, 80, 91, 140, 168
Gifford, Denis 171, 173
Gladstone, William 54
Gordon Highlanders Leaving for the Boer War (1899) 43, **44**
Grand National (1899) 50, **51**
Grandma's Reading Glass (1900) 149, **153**

Great Northern Railway Works at Doncaster (1900) 91
Green, Tom 122, 140, 150, 161, 172

Haggar's Bioscope Camera (c. 1900) **63**, 86
Hanging out the Clothes (1897) 29
Haunted Curiosity Shop, The (1901) **134**, 135
Haunted Picture Gallery, The 119, 171
Haverstraw Tunnel (1897) 98
Hawthorne, Lil 168, 169, 172
Haydon and Urry 86, 144, 147
He and She (1898) 145, 146
Hepworth, Cecil 18, 19, 58, 70, 86, 89, 90, 100, 102, 103, 105, 118, 122, 136, 138, 139, 141, 144, 145, 163
Her Majesty the Queen Arriving at South Kensington on the Occasion of the Laying of the Foundation Stone of The Victorian and Albert Museum (1899) 112
Herbert Campbell as Little Bobby (1899) 131, 140, **153**
Hindoo Jugglers (1900) 130
Hindoo Snake Charmer Performing the Mango (1901) 172
homme de têtes, Un (1898) 132
Honri, Perci 130
House that Jack Built, The (1900) 137, **137**
How it Feels to be Run Over (1900) 138
Hull Fair (1902) 87

Incident at Clovelly Cottage (1895) 31
Indian Chief and the Seidlitz Powder (1901) 138
Irish Mail Taking up Water (1898) **108**
Irish Mail Taking up Water at Full Speed, The (1898) 99, **99**

Kidnapped by Indians (1899) 165
King John (1899) 157, **157**
Kiss in the Tunnel, The (1899) 30, 33, 100, 146, 147, **147**
Kitty Mahone (1900) 168, **169**, 172
Kruger's Dream of Empire (1900) 71

Landing an Old Lady from a Small Boat or *Lady and the Boat* (1899) 144
Landing of Savage South Africa at Southampton, The (1899) 48
Last Days of Pompeii, The (1900) 136
Launch of H.M.S. Albion, The (Paul, 1898) 36–7, **36**
Launch of H.M.S. Albion, The (Prestwich, 1898) **35**, 36
Launch of the Oceanic (1898) **63**
Launch of the Worthing Lifeboat (1898) **58**, 59
Launch of the Worthing Lifeboat: Coming Ashore (1898) **118**, 119
Leno, Dan 28, 31
Let Me Dream Again (1900) 30, 149
Liverpool v Small Heath (1901) 52
Liverpool v. Small Heath (1901) 54
Lobengula, Peter 48, 49
Lord Roberts Hoisting the Union Flag at Pretoria (1900) 45
Lover Kisses Husband (1900) 146
Low, Rachael 101, 163, 173
Lubin, Siegmund 170
Lumière Company 17, 20, 21, 22, 26, 55, 67, 86, 96, 98, 100, 104, 117, 129, 159, 171

Magic Extinguisher, The (1901) **128**
Magic Sword, The (1901) 172
Making Sausages; or the End of All Things (1897) 171
Manchester and Salford Harriers' Cyclists Procession (1901) 90
Manchester Street Scenes (1901) 90
Mary Jane's Mishap (1903) 147
Maskelyne, John Nevil 122, 123, 128, 129
Maskelyne, Nevil 30, 122
Maxim Firing Field Gun (1897) **70**, 71
Me and My Two Friends (1898) 60, **60**
Méliès, Georges 124, 128, 129, 132, 160, 162
Mesmerist, The (1898) 134, 161
Miller and the Sweep, The (1897) 142, **143**
Miners Leaving Pendlebury Colliery (1901) 49, **49**
Miss Bayley (1900) 130
Mitchell and Kenyon 48, 49, 52, 65, 78, 80, 81, 82, 84, 85, 86, 87, 90, 94, 100, 105, 117, 130, 164, 173, 178
Morning Wash, A (1900) 80–1, **81**
Mr Moon (1900) **130**, 131
Mysterious Rabbit, The (1896) 129
Mystic Chamber, The (c.1897) 133

Nankin Road, Shanghai (1900) 45, 72–3, **73**
Negro Women Coaling a Vessel (1901) 172
North Sea Fisheries, North Shields (1901) 92, **92**
Norton, Charles Goodwin 56, 124
Nurses on the Battlefield (1899) 164

Octopus, The (1901) 171
Old Maid's Valentine (1900) 140, **141**
Old Man Drinking a Glass of Beer (1897) 140
On a Runaway Motor Car through Piccadilly Circus (1897) 100
Our Army 70
Our Navy (1898) 68–9, **68**, 70, 89, 90, 156

Panorama – Highgate Tunnel – Goods train (1895) 171
Panorama around the Eiffel Tower (1900) 104
Panorama de Westminster pris de la Tamise (1897) 100
Panorama du Grand Canal pris d'un bateau (1896) 96
Panorama of Ealing from a Moving Tram (1901) 106, **109**
Panorama of the Druidical Monuments at Stonehenge (1900) 102, **102**
Panorama of the Paris Exhibition (1900) 103, **103**
Panorama Taken in a Steam Crane (1900) 171
Panoramic View of Conway on the L. & N.W Railway (1898) **97**, 99, 119
Panoramic View of the Vegetable Market at Venice (1898) 100, **101**, 103
Paul, Robert William 11, 12, 16, 18, **19**, 20, 23, 27, 28, 30, 31, 32, 33, 36, 37, 39, 50, 62, 70, 71, 86, 90, 100, 101, 105, 106, 111, 114, 117, 124, 126, 128, 130, 132, 134, 135, 136, 146, 149, 150, 151, 152, 156, 157, 159, 160, 162, 163, 164, 165, 179, 180
Pelicans in the Zoo (1898) 120, **120**
Photograph Taken from our Area Window (1901) 148
Photographing a Ghost (1898) 133, 161
Photographing the Audience (1901) 170
Plucked from the Burning (1900) 136

Policeman and the Cook or the Copper in the Copper (1898) 146
Pope Leo XIII Leaving Carriage and Being Ushered into Garden (1898) **14, 15**
Portrait, or the Soldier's Dream of Home (1900) 164
Prestwich Film Company 36, 62, 84, 95, 117, 173
Promio, Alexander 96, 97, 100, 117
Puzzled Bather and His Animated Clothes, The (1901) **136**, 137

Queen Victoria's Diamond Jubilee (Prestwich, 1897) **38**
Queen Victoria's Diamond Jubilee – Queen in Carriage (1897) **110**
Queen Victoria's Diamond Jubilee (British Cinematographe, 1897) 9, **9**
Queen Victoria's Last Visit to Ireland (1900) **41**
Quick Change Act (1908) 130

Railway Collision, A (1900) 136, 165, 166, **166**
Repairing the Broken Bridge at Frere (1899) 75
Rescue from Drowning (1898) 159
Rescued by Rover (1905) 138
Return of the Warwickshire Regiment (1902) 78–9, **78**
Ride on a Tram through Belfast 106
Ride on the Peak Tramway (1900) 45, 105, **109**
Rifle Hill Signal Corps (1899) 75, **75**
Riley Brothers 56, 146
Rip Van Winkle (1896) 158, 160, 163
Rosenthal, Joseph 33, 45, 64, 72, 77, 105
Rough Sea at Dover (1895) 22, 55, 56, 114, 115
Rough Seas Breaking on Rocks (1899) **114**
Rudge and Whitworth, Britain's Best Bicycle (c. 1901) **124**, 125

Sailor's Departure, The (1898) 160
Sailors Return, The (1898) 160
Santa Claus (1898) 62, **63**, 161
Savage South Africa: Attack and Repulse (1899) 48
Scenes at Balmoral (1896) **10**
Scrooge; or, Marley's Ghost (1901) 62, **155**, 156, 160, 162, 163
Sea Cave Near Lisbon, A (1896) 101, **116**, 117
Sedgwick's Bioscope Showfront at Pendlebury Wakes (1901) 87, **87**
Sheffield Photo Company 163
Signing of the Peace at Vereeniging (1902) 164
Smith, George Albert 11, 12, 18, **19**, 29, 30, 33, 56, 62, 100, 104, 119, 120, 122, 128, 130, 132, 133, 134, 136, 140, 142, 146, 147, 148, 149, 151, 160, 161, 170
Snapshotting an Audience (1900) 151, 170
Sneaky Boer, A (1900) 164
Solar Eclipse (1900) 122–3, **123**
Soldier's Courtship, The (1896) 23, **24**, 146
Sortie des usines à Lyon (1895) 22
Spiders on a Web (1900) 120, **121**
Spirit of his Forefathers, The (1900) 119, **124**, 125
Stanford, John Benett 64
Stop Thief! (1901) 149, 163
Street Scene in Boar Lane, Leeds 59
Surf at Long Branch (1896) 56

Thames River Scenery – Panorama of the Crowded River (1899) **109**
Thames River Scenery (1900) 102
Thomas, Arthur Duncan   27, 37, 81, 88, **88**, 89, **89**, 90, 95
Through Chiselhurst Tunnel on the S.E.R.   100
Torpedo Flottila visit to Manchester (1901)   **89**, 90
Trafalgar Day in Liverpool (1901)   48, **72**
Tram Ride through Southampton (1900)   **109**
Trewey, Félicien   26, 128, 129
Trip to Vesuvius (1901)   **63**, **106**, **108**
Twelve Months Later   148
Two A.M. or the Husband's Return (1896)   146
Two Laughing Men (1900)   140, **153**
Two Old Sports (1900)   140

Upside Down, or the Human Flies (1899)   126, **127**
Urban, Charles   18, **19**, 29, 33, 79, 80, 89, 91, 104, 172
Vaulting Horses (1900)   **69**, 70

Velograph Company   39
Victoria, Queen   10, 11, 33, 38, 39, 42, 43, 54, 64, 68, 79, 96, 111, 112, 125, 162
View from an Engine Front – Barnstaple (1898)   **108**
View from an Engine Front – Shilla Mill Tunnel (1898)   100, **108**
View from an Engine Front – Train Leaving Tunnel (1898)   100
Vinolia Soap (1898)   124

Visit to Pompeii (1901)   104, **105**
Voyage dans la Lune, Le (1902)   139

W. G. Grace Filoscope Film (c.1899)   **63**
Waller, Lewis   157
Walturdaw Company   33
Warwick Trading Company   29, 32, 43, 45, 48, 52, 70, 72, 80, 81, 104, 105, 117, 133, 162, 165, 166, 171, 172
Washing the Sweep (1898)   144
Watkins, Robert Lincoln   120
Wells, Herbert George   106
West, Alfred   68, 70, 89, 90
Whisky of His Ancestors (1899)   124, 125
White, James   56, 104
Will Evans the Musical Eccentric (1899)   29
Williams, Randall   86, 87, 160
Williamson, James   11, 12, 18, **19**, 61, 73, 132, 136, 144, 149, 150, 151, 163, 166
Woman Undressing (c.1896)   **63**, 148, 149
Workers at Kynoch Ltd. Lion Works, Birmingham (1901)   91
Workforce Leaving Alfred Butterworth and Sons, Glebe Mills (1901)   94–5, **94**
Works and Workers of Denton Holme (1910)   86
Wrench, Alfred   39, 111

Youdale, William Henry   117

Zola Rochefort Duel, The (1898)   157

ILLUSTRATION CREDITS

While considerable effort has been made to correctly identify copyright holders, this has not been possible in all cases. Where no rights holder is listed, the image is understood to be out of copyright. Any omissions or corrections brought to our attention will be remedied in any future editions. The majority of images are sourced from digitised films from the BFI National Archive.

p. 19 Portraits of R. W. Paul, G. A. Smith, Birt Acres, James Williamson, Cecil Hepworth, Charles Urban, all from BFI Stills, Posters and Designs; **p. 24** *The Soldier's Courtship*, courtesy of Archivio Fotografico della Cineteca Nazionale Centro Sperimentale di Cinematografia; **p. 32** Warwick Trading Co. Catalogue from BFI Reuben Library; **p. 40** map of the route of Queen Victoria's Diamond Jubilee procession showing positions of cameramen, adapted and updated from an original composite image created by Luke McKernan, using original image sourced from Souvenir Jubilee brochure held at BFI National Archive; **p. 42** *Queen Victoria's Last Visit to Ireland*, courtesy of Museum of Modern Art Film Department; **p. 53** 'Birt Acres Filming the Derby', from BFI Stills, Posters and Designs; **p. 68** photograph of Alfred West filming *Our Navy*, from the collection of A. S. Clover (1917–1998), courtesy of David Clover; **p. 70** *Maxim, Firing Field Gun*, courtesy of Museum of Modern Art Film Department; **p. 97** *Panoramic View of Conway Castle on the L. & N. W. Railway*, courtesy of Eye Filmmuseum; **p. 109** *Panorama of Ealing from a Moving Tram*, courtesy of Museum of Modern Art Film Department; **p. 123** *Solar Eclipse*, courtesy of the Royal Astronomical Society; **p. 147** *The Kiss in the Tunnel*, from BFI Stills, Posters and Designs; **p. 157** *King John*, courtesy of EYE Filmmuseum.

BFI BRITISH SCREEN STORIES

THE BRITISH SCREEN STORIES series provides a unique guide to significant and sometimes overlooked stories from the history of British film and television. Rooted in, and richly illustrated with, material from the BFI National Archive, the books lead readers through this fascinating terrain, expanding our understanding of familiar stories and enabling the discovery of those less well-known.

Each book focuses on a different aspect of British film and television and is written in an authoritative yet accessible style. Extensive use of stills and other archive materials that tell new stories about our screen heritage complement the text. Distinctive elements are the 'close-up' and 'montage' features interspersing each book. These features illustrate a particular topic, technique or aesthetic development with a concise, direct and strong visual narrative approach.

OTHER TITLES IN THIS SERIES

PUBLISHED
The Story of British Animation by **Jez Stewart**

FORTHCOMING
The Story of British Propaganda Film by **Scott Anthony**
The Story of Video Activism by **Ed Webb-Ingall**
The Story of British Screen Advertising by **Emily Caston**
The Story of British Sport on Screen by **Paul Wells**
The Story of Industrial and Corporate Film by **Patrick Russell**

Queries, ideas and submissions to the series editors:
Mark Duguid – Mark.Duguid@bfi.org.uk
Patrick Russell – Patrick.Russell@bfi.org.uk